Fuerteventura

Travel with
Insider
Tips

How this Guide Works

Our guide introduces you to the sights on Fuerteventura (and neighbouring Lanzarote) in four chapters. The map below presents an overview of how the chapters are arranged. Each one has been allocated a special colour. In order to help you plan your trip, we have subdivided all the main points of interest in each chapter into three sections: the must-see sights are listed under the *TOP 10* and also highlighted in the book with two stars. You'll find other important sites that didn't quite make our *Top 10* list in the *Don't Miss* section. A selection of other places worth seeing appears in the *At Your Leisure* section.

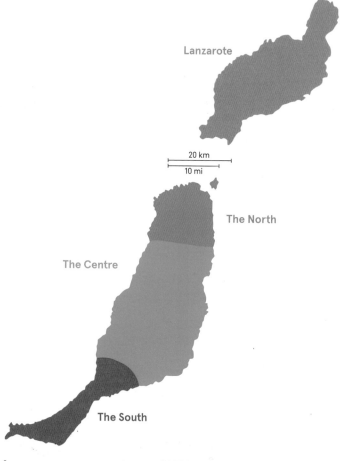

Lanzarote

20 km
10 mi

The North

The Centre

The South

The picturesque natural harbour of El Cotillo; in the background is the Torre El Tostón, a lookout tower from the 18th century.

The perfect scenic viewpoint, the Mirador del Rio in the north of Lanzarote is always good for a photo or a selfie.

TOP 10

★★ TOP 10

Not to be missed! Our top hits – from the absolute No. 1 to No. 10 – help you plan your tour of the most important sights.

❶ ★★ Jandía Playa & Morro Jable
Fuerteventura's beach paradise is the main reason that millions of tourists flock to this island in the sun every year (p. 108).

❷ ★★ Betancuria
The old capital retains its colonial flair and is one of the most popular day-trip destinations on the island (p. 78).

❸ ★★ Antigua
A windmill forms the hub of a museum complex that also includes a botanic garden and a crafts centre (p. 82).

❹ ★★ Isla de Lobos
It is possible to explore the uninhabited island just off the north coast by booking a boat trip combined with a walking tour. The highlight is climbing the Montaña Caldera volcano (p. 48).

❺ ★★ Corralejo
A popular holiday destination on the north of the island is Corralejo; stretching along the coast to the south is a magnificent dune and beach landscape. At

sunrise, the dunes look absolutely amazing (p. 51).

❻ ★★ La Oliva
In the north, the fortified Casa de los Coroneles provides an excellent view of the island's turbulent past (p. 55).

❼ ★★ Ecomuseo de La Alcogida
In the intricately and lovingly designed open-air museum, five beautifully restored farmhouses and *artesanías* demonstrate how the rural population used to live (p. 84).

❽ ★★ La Lajita Oasis Park
The large zoo, embedded in what for Fuerteventura could almost be classed as lush subtropical vegetation, attracts visitors with big game and animal shows (p. 113).

❾ ★★ Parque Nacional Timanfaya
A day trip to the neighbouring island of Lanzarote introduces you to the wonderful volcanic legacy of the Canary Islands (p. 138).

❿ ★★ Jameos del Agua
The highlights of the fantasy grotto created by César Manrique inside this lava tube are a Caribbean-style pool and a cave-based auditorium famous for its fantastic acoustics (p. 142).

That Fuerteventura Feeling

Find out what makes
the island tick,
experience its unique flair –
just like the *Majoreros*
themselves.

Wind and Waves

Visit Fuerteventura and you will experience the sea at its best. You will not find such broad open beaches on any of the other Canary Islands. Granted, a few of them are slightly disfigured by unattractive hotel complexes, but on the unspoiled Playa de Barlovento, you can sometimes walk for hours barefoot along the edge of the water without meeting a soul, enjoying the sea breeze, the lapping of the waves against the shore and the screeching of the seagulls circling above you.

Pure Relaxation to Recharge your Batteries

The South (p. 98) of Fuerteventura, from Costa Calma to Morro Jable, is still relatively uncharted territory for tourists. Just 40 years ago, apart from two tiny fishing hamlets, there was practically no tourist infrastructure here at all. There may be no cultural highlights for your photo album in the south of the island, but you can swim, surf, dive, wander along the beaches, meditate or simply relax by the hotel pool and read a novel.

That Sahara Feeling

The dunes of Corralejo (p. 54) save you a trip to the Sahara. The constant wind has piled up towering hills of sand which offer a particularly impressive view of the wonders of nature on a morning walk or in the soft light just before sunset. Against this background, the tall Riu hotels – built in the 1970s when this expansive area was not yet protected – give the impression of a Fata Morgana mirage that you can simply block out of your mind's eye.

The huge expanse of sand, gentle waves and a light wind are an open invitation to stroll along the beach near Corralejo.

A ring of stones provides some protection from the wind and a sheltered place to relax.

Many beach restaurants serve excellent fish dishes and have a view of the sea.

The capital Betancuria is characterised by its tranquility, its atmosphere and its colonial flair.

How about a Volcano walk?

You are missing something if you regard Fuerteventura as just a beach holiday destination. There are countless wonderful ways to explore the island on foot. For instance, the well marked Sendero de Bayuyo (p. 164) trail leads you on an excursion through the bizarre Malpaís de Bayuyo lava field. You can view the volcanic past of the island first-hand and look down into the crater of Calderón Hondo.

Open Invitation to a Fish Restauant on the Seafront

What could be nicer after enjoying the sand than to round off the day in a small fish restaurant with good food and a glass of wine, perhaps with the added bonus of a breathtaking sunset? There are plenty of places to do this along the 300km (186mi)-long coast around Fuerteventura. The largest choice is offered on the promenade of Morro Jable which is lined with restaurants; you are in good hands at the Saavedra Clavijo (p. 125), which serves a lavish paella with fresh shellfish. But other – often simple easteries – also serve fresh fish too and well-chilled wines.

Colonial Flair

Compared with the main islands of Gran Canaria and Tenerife, the colonial heritage on Fuerteventura is relatively modest. Yet in some places, the past is still alive here, too, especially in the old capital of Betancuria (p. 78). There, you enter the parish church Santa Maria from the 17th century through an attractive Renaissance portal, and cosy restaurants have been set up in the old mansion houses, such as Casa Santa Maria (p. 79) right opposite the church.

Say Cheese

Until just a few years ago, there were more goats than humans living on Fuerteventura. Even today, of all the Canary Islands, Fuerte remains the one associated with goats. The much prized goat's cheese is extremely popular in many of the restaurants, both by the locals as well as tourists. It usually comes fried and with *mojo* sauce. Refined with sweet paprika or *gofio*, the cheese has a unique flavour. Sometimes it is also smoked and served together with air-dried ham. A good place to sample the different varieties is in the Betancuria cheese factory (p. 96).

A wonderful panoramic view of the sea and Cardon mountain opens up near the small village of Corrales de las Hermosas.

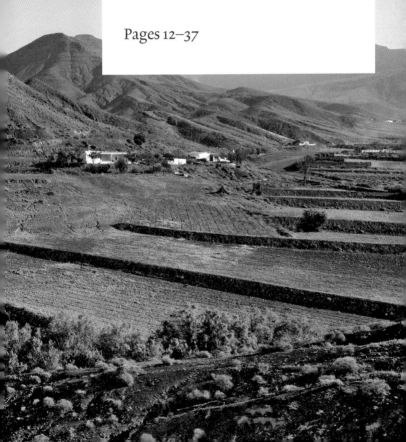

The Magazine

Soaking up the sun, walking along beaches, diving, surfing and simply enjoying the sea – Fuerteventura, however, has much more to offer.

Pages 12–37

The Desert Island

Of the seven main islands that make up the Canaries, Fuerteventura is the classic desert island. It is often referred to as 'a little bit of the Sahara which has been chipped off the coast of Africa' – that is of course geologically incorrect. Like all the Canaries it was formed through the collision of the European and the African plates.

Even the golden yellow sand on the beaches was not, as is often incorrectly claimed, blown over from the Sahara but is actually 'home-made'. For visitors much of the island offers a magnificent untamed natural beauty: ancient mountain ranges and volcanic cones trimmed by deep, dry *barrancos* (ravines), and the coast, with its sand dunes formed by the trade winds, seems almost African. Less attractively, there are also great stretches of volcanic *malpais* (literally, badlands), black areas of scorched, cracked earth where nothing more than a few species of plants such as thorn bushes, the gorse-like *Launaea arborescens* and lichens grow. For the islanders this has always been a harsh, unforgiving climate in which to eke a living. However, *majoreros*, as the people of Fuerteventura are colloquially known, are nothing if not resourceful.

Back in the 18th century, windmills were used by farmers to grind corn into flour, while animal-power brought well-water up to the surface. In the burning sun, opuntia and some species of sisal flourish, while the former wide-spread cultivation of tomatoes has more or less been abandoned. Camels, once used as working animals, are seldom to be found on the fields today. These tireless 'ships of the desert' can only be seen now in the Oasis Park in La Lajita (p. 113). More recently, the medicinal plant aloe vera, that survives very well in this dry, island climate and needs little water, has been planted more intensively.

Meeting new challenges

A structural change in the 1970s led to the island's development into a holiday resort. Fuerteventura's greatest capital is to be found in its mile-long sandy beaches and within a relatively short time the

Fuerteventura is covered by large, barren areas of volcanic origin.

island evolved into one of the most popular beach-holiday destinations in Europe. Since then, tourism has filled the coffers in the town halls of the local communities – and

nothing now remains of the former poorhouse of the Canaries that the island once was. In addition to the swimmers and surfers, an increasing number of golf tourists come to the island as well as visitors from cruise liners. In total, more than two million guests visit the island every year. Tourism attracted a large work force from the Spanish mainland and migrant workers from central Europe to Fuerteventura: and since1990 the population has now trebled.

Having managed to survive on a basic economy since before the days of the Conquest, the islanders' latest challenge is how to reap the benefits of tourism without sowing the seeds of cultural destruction. The success of *casas rurales* and *hoteles rurales* (rural guesthouses and hotels), as well as projects such as the Ecomuseo de La Alcogida open-air museum, are seen by many to be the most appropriate routes for controlled tourist development. Yet the growing number of holiday resorts in tourist magnets such as Jandía and Corralejo, not to mention the plans for hollowing out the island's most sacred mountain as a tourist attraction, are of great concern to many islanders and Canarian conservationists. For the moment, at least, most of Fuerteventura remains, in the words of the poet Miguel Unamuno, 'an oasis in the desert of civilization'.

Ideal conditions for kiteboarders can be found on the Playa Barca near Costa Calma.

Blowing in the Wind

Letting the wind blow in your face – that's something you will certainly feel on Fuerteventura! The reason for this is the northeast trade wind that sends a strong current of air to the Canary Islands on more than 300 days a year from the weather cauldron in the Azores.

When the trade winds take a break, generally in the winter months, your have the feeling that something is missing. Windsurfers and kiteboarders seek out the shade of the beach bars and wait until the wind picks up again. But no wind, as mentioned above, is not the norm.

Fuerteventura without wind is just as unthinkable as a desert without sand – and there is a lot of the latter on the second largest of the Canary Islands, too. The name of the island itself reflects nature's dominance: *fuerte* = Spanish for 'strong'; *ventus* = Latin for 'wind'. The wind is not just something for surfers or for beach hikers who like a strong breeze, summer and winter; it is also an element that has shaped Fuerteventura's landscape. Sand dunes higher than houses rise up behind most of the mile-long beaches. In Corralejo Natural Park, the wind blows sand across the roads that then have to be dug out by a bulldozer. You can hike through the dunes that are up to 20m (65ft) high in this conservation area that stretches over an area of more than 2600 hectares (6500 acres). The following day you will find that your footprints have disappeared. And if you come back again next year you will see that the dunes themselves have shifted – everything here is on the move.

Fuerteventura's windmills, however, are no longer in use – at least not in their original function. Well into the 20th century, the mills ground the flour needed to make *gofio* (p. 29), the staple food eaten daily by Canarios. There used to be some three dozen windmills scattered over the island - Don Quixote would have had a whale of a time! Alongside these, grist mills powered by animals, either mules or camels, were to be found in the vicinity. The change to electrically-driven mills happened more or

less overnight. As a result, the old windmills fell into disrepair and became ruins in the landscape with little more than the foundations left standing. If was only after the island's rise in popularity as a beach-holiday destination that enough money became available to invest in the area's heritage and restore one mill or another – that have since become tourist attractions.

On the 'Ruta de los Molinos', the mill route from Tefía to Tiscamanita, some half a dozen windmills can be

Molina de Tefia on the 'Ruta de los Molinas'

seen near the roadside that have now been restored. Unfortunately their sails have been anchored and do not turn in the wind, but they can be seen from miles around and form picturesque eye-catchers in an otherwise desolate landscape. The windmill in Antigua (p. 82) can be visited inside and, in the mill museum in Tiscamanita, the complete mill machinery can be viewed.

Guanches, Majores and Conquistadores

When the Norman baron Jean de Béthencourt first arrived on Fuerteventura in 1402, a curious sight awaited him. Here were a people only slightly removed from the Stone Age in appearance and technology.

They lived together, just a few hundred strong, in primitive societies with basic laws and rough draconian justice; convicted criminals' skulls were crushed by heavy rocks, for example. Yet it is also recorded that they were a peaceful people with high moral standards; Béthencourt's priests chronicled, 'go throughout the world and nowhere will you find a finer and better formed people...with great minds were they to receive instructions' (Bontier & le Verrier, tr. and ed, *Le Canarien*, 1872).

The history books came to call them Guanches ('gwanches') but in fact this term is a general one for any aboriginal Canary Island dweller and the ancient people of Fuerteventura came to be known as

The French explorer Jean de Béthencourt was also referred to as the King of the Canary Islands.

Betancuria is the former capital of Fuerteventura. Its name is derived from Béthencourt who, in the service of the Spanish crown, conquered the island.

majoreros (pronounced 'ma-ho-rair-os') or Mahohreros, possibly named after the particular types of caves *(majos)* that they built, or from the word *mahos* meaning a type of goat-skin shoe which they wore.

The Origin of the Guanches

It is thought that these original islanders were of Berber origin, coming from Morocco in Roman times (carbon-dating points to the 1st or 2nd century BC) and they may have been from the Canarii tribe, hence the subsequent name of the archipelago. They dwelt in caves and in low houses (as many villagers do today), kept goats, ate shellfish and grain, made simple pottery and tattooed themselves in geometrical patterns with pottery stamps known as *pintaderas*. These were probably also used to distinguish ownership of pots in grain stores.

The island was divided into two kingdoms: Jandía (as it is today), ruled by King Guize, and Maxorata (the rest of the island), ruled by King Ayoze. Béthencourt recorded that a low wall, around a metre high, crossed the island at La Pared dividing the two kingdoms. Traces of it can still be found today and there may have been defensive turrets in place.

Spain's Gain

Had the French court supported the Norman explorer Jean de Béthencourt, the inhabitants of the Canary Islands would probably be speaking French today. However, the French refused to finance Béthencourt's project and thus the knight took his request to Castile. There, he was told that he would receive support only if the islands subsequently became part of the Spanish empire.

Béthencourt thus travelled to the islands, to discover new land and resources for Castile. The job of the missionaries accompanying him was to convert the natives to Christianity. Frustrated in meeting either of these aims and encountering strong resistance from the islanders, the French nobleman sailed back to his Castilian sponsors for reinforcements.

Fuerteventura Becomes an Outpost of Castile

When Béthencourt returned with his conquistadors in 1404 he found that the islanders had built forts at Valtarajal (later known as Betancuria) and Rico Roque (close to El Cotillo), but armed with merely spears and staves against guns they were soon overcome. Some fled into the mountains before giving themselves up to be sold into slavery abroad. Many died of common diseases imported by the invaders. In January 1405, the two kings surrendered and the

The Idol of Tara, an artwork produced by the Guanches, in the Museo Canario

remaining islanders followed their example.

Compared with the islands of Gran Canaria and La Palma, the original inhabitants of Fuerteventura have left few traces. Ceramic shards and a few stone idols may be seen in the Museo Arqueológico at Betancuria but the best-known site associated with the ancient inhabitants is Montaña de Tindaya. If was here that unusual prehistoric rock engravings depicting the shapes of feet (Spanish: *podomorfos*) were discovered. Their exact purpose is still to be thoroughly researched and, as such, remains a secret of the lost culture of the Guanche people.

Fuerte for the Fit and Fun-Loving

That Fuerteventura, with its mile-long beaches and reliable wind, has become a hotspot for water sports enthusiasts, is nothing of a secret today. It provides perfect conditions for windsurfers and kiteboarders as well as classic surfers. However, away from the wind and the waves, Fuerteventura is very good for hiking, mountainbiking and golf. Large holiday complexes also have diving bases and offer courses in catamaran sailing and archery.

Trade winds and the big waves make Fuerteventura a surfer's paradise

It's basically down to geography. The Canary Islands have always benefited (and suffered) from heavy swells and strong winds. Ancient mariners relied on these 'trade winds' to speed their voyages, and water sports fans also look for strong and reliable breezes. This is where the 'acceleration zones' come in. These occur where the wind is funnelled between mountains or small islands and can triple the wind in strength. Because of its location, Fuerteventura – in particular the Sotavento coast of Jandía and the northern coast around Corralejo – benefits from this effect.

Windsurfing, the Island's Top Sport
Windsurfing has made Fuerteventura internationally famous and in July 1986 the first Windsurfing World Cup competition was held on Playa Barca (p. 117). Since the windsurfing and kiteboarding world championships in 2001, World Cup

The south of Fuerteventura, here Playas de Sotavento, is a kiteboarder's paradise.

competitions, attracting many spectators, have been held on Sotavento beach every year. Large windsurfing centres cater to every sport enthusiast's needs and stock all necessary equipment. While professionals value the strong winds in the summer, the winter months are recommended for beginners when the trade winds die down.

Lots of practice is necessary before you can surf properly.

Fuerteventura is also renowned for its classical (wave) surfing. Especially good conditions can be found off the coast at La Pared (p. 119). Surf camps teach budding surfers the necessities until one is good enough to stand more or less upright on a board! And, of course. stand-up paddling arrived on Fuerteventura some time ago. You can hire boards for this trendy, easy-to-learn sport from many places along the coast.

Fantastic views can be enjoyed on every hike.

Beach and Vulcano Hikes

There are few places quite so stunning to go for a walk: mile-long sandy beaches and paths along the coastline against a backdrop of cliffs bizarrely formed by the wind and waves are an open invitation to a hike. In addition, the local government has waymarked a number of stretches inland as well.

While Fuerteventura cannot compete with classic (green) hikers' island such as Tenerife, La Palma or La Gomera, Fuerteventura's barren landscape with its mountains coloured anything from ochre to brown, is particularly appealing to many hikers. The short hike from the Barranco de las Peñitas or the climb up Pico de la Zarza (p. 112) are especially attractive, with the latter having a difference in altitude of 800m (2625ft). The volcano path from the crater Calderón Hondo and the circular route around the island of Lobos have become popular tours. (For a detailed description, see p. 160).

Cycling and Mountainbiking

A lot has been done over the past few years to cater for the demands of cyclists. Several roads are now accompanied by separate cycle paths. Inland, there are countless roads that are relatively seldom used by cars that are good and safe for cyclists. Nevertheless, the constant wind can make headway difficult.

Mountainbikers can find demanding off-road routes primarily in the area around Corralejo. However, to protect the fragile ecosystem, you should never leave the waymarked tracks. Las Playitas (p. 93) is the perfect spot for the dedicated cyclist. As the island's major cycling hub where triathletes and professional cyclists train, group excursions are organised several times a week for road racing cyclists and for mountainbikers.

Tennis and Golf

Tennis can be played at many of the larger hotels. Holiday clubs such as Robinson and Aldiana cater for both beginners and experienced players and offer lessons and

Fuerteventura can easily be explored by bike, either on a mountainbike for the more athletic or a touring bike.

Golf players have to cope with both the sun and the wind at the Golf Club Salinas de Antigua.

Triathletes competing near Gran Tarajal

organise competitions for visitors. The Robinson Club Esquinzo Playa, for example, has eleven sand courts. If you like, you can also play there by floodlight in the evenings. You don't necessarily have to bring your own racket.

Golf on a desert island? Environmentalists and ecologists are tearing their hair out over the watering of the greens alone. Looking after the four 18-hole couses on Fuerteventura really does use a lot of water. The operators use seawater and run their own desalination plants. These in turn, however, require a huge amount of energy.

Carnival and Fiesta

The Canary Islands celebrate the traditional pre-Lent carnival, or *carnaval* as it is known in Spain, with every ounce of energy they can muster. Neighbouring Gran Canaria and Tenerife compete to stage the biggest parades this side of Rio, while the other islands do their very best to keep pace.

The biggest *carnaval* celebrations on Fuerteventura are in Corralejo and Puerto del Rosario, though it is celebrated with gusto all over the island. The dates vary from year to year, but it all starts around nine weeks before Easter (usually early to mid-February) with the *Verbena de la Sábana* (Sheet Party) for which participants dress in a sheet and little else. After this the Carnival Queen and the Children's Queen are elected.

Among the highlights of the festivities is the election of the Drag Queen – a man dressed up as a woman – and the large and colourful procession through the streets (*Concurso de Murgas*) that generally takes place in Puerto del Rosario on the Saturday during carnival time. Street parties and processions shimmy and shake to the insistent beat of salsa, lubricated by a seemingly inexhaustible supply of *cuba libre* (rum, cola, lime juice and ice)

served from street kiosks. One typical carnival event is held in Puerto del Rosario on the Sunday, beyond

Everyone puts on fancy dress and parties in the street

Spectacular processions take place at carnival time with elaborate costumes and colourful decorations that are a feast for the eyes.

the harbour wall – the *Regata de Achipenco*. The weird and wonderful vessels are made of all sorts of bits and pieces. No engines are allowed nor any flotation devices used on conventional boats and ships. The winner is not the fastest but the one with the most imaginatively designed vessel and the team with the wackiest costumes.

The Burial of the Sardine

A feature of *carnaval* is that men always dress in drag. If you think that is odd wait until you see the strangest ceremony of all, the Burial of the Sardine, which symbolises the end of *carnaval* and the beginning of Lent, as well as the Lenten

fast and abstinence. On Ash Wednesday a huge papier-maché sardine is carried in a mock funeral procession through the streets accompanied by the bizarre sight and sound of black-clad 'mourners' wailing and crying. When the sardine arrives at its appointed place at the harbour, fireworks inside the fish are lit and it is literally blown to pieces.

Festivities in Honour of the Virgin Mary

Island fiestas commemorate the feast day of the local saint or the Virgin/Our Lady, *(Nuestra Señora)*. The centrepiece is a procession with prominent parishioners carrying an effigy of the saint or the Virgin shoulder-high through the streets accompanied by troupes of local musicians in traditional dress. The more important fiestas will also have carnival-style floats, street food and stalls, and culminate in fireworks. One of the island's most important fiestas is the Romería (pilgrimage) to the Ermita of the Virgen de la Peña, the patron saint of the island, in Vega de Río Palmas on the third weekend in September.

The Fiesta de Nuestra Señora del Carmen on 16 July at Corralejo and Morro Jable pays homage to the patron saint of fishermen with colourful boat processions led by local fishermen carrying a statue of the Virgin.

On the third Sunday in August, the old harbour at El Cotillo is dotted with boats celebrating Nuestra Señora del Buen Viaje.

Fuerteventura 1 England 0

On 13 October the locals celebrate the day they gave the English a bloody nose in 1740 by re-enacting the Battle of Tamasite, near Tuineje. A troop of well-armed English privateers (state-sanctioned pirates) attacked near Tuineje and was seen off by a group of 37 locals with muskets and agricultural tools. Thirty Englishmen were killed and five locals died. A cannon was captured and is on display outside the archaeological museum in Betancuria. A painting in the church of Tuineje also recalls the victory.

Almost the whole local population is out in the street when the procession to honour Nuestra Señora de la Candelaria takes place in Gran Tarajal.

Gofio, Mojo and Wrinkly Potatoes

There is no typical Fuerteventura-cuisine –
but there is very much a Canarian one.
It is down-to-earth and is made up of
produce grown locally and what the
sea provides. That is not an awful lot but
more than you perhaps think for a semi-desert
island. The local food is unique at any
rate – so just give it a try.

In most restaurants and at hotel buffets in the tourist centres you will seldom find local fare. The focus is entirely on the tastes of the guests who come from all corners of Europe. Typical international food is served, ranging from pasta to pizza and from steak to lamb chops. You are most likely to be lucky in eateries in small villages well away from the tourist areas where few foreigners stray to such as Gran Tarajal, Pájara or Villaverde.

Classic, Simple and Good

Papas arrugadas are so-to-speak the be-all and end-all of Canarian fare and *the* vegetable to accompany fish and meat dishes. Wrinkly potatoes are so called as their skin wrinkles when boiled in water with added sea salt. The skin is always eaten as well. There is often a salt crust on it – so don't add any extra salt! A *mojo* sauce is always served with wrinkly potatoes that is a different colour to whatever else is on the plate: *mojo verde* – a green sauce with lots of coriander is usually served with fish, for example, whereas *mojo rojo*, made of red (paprika) peppers, accompanies meat dishes. Both have a lot of olive oil in them and cooks are never stingy with the garlic. Every restaurant that takes any pride in its food, makes its own *mojo*. Supermarkets, however, do stock ready-made products.

Looking at the shelves in any supermarket you will notice another item essential to the Canarian

Gofio is also served as a kind of porridge and mixed into soups.

Paella is a true feast for the senses.

Canarian fare without fish or seafood is unthinkable.

cuisine: *gofio*. Even the original islanders ground barley using simple handmills to make flour which they mixed with water or goat's milk into a nourishing porridge. Today, the flour is generally made from wheat and maize. *Gofio* is more or less a Canarian polenta. It is often added to soups and stews, mixed into dough or muesli, made into ice-cream or, with a dollop of whipped cream, eggs, ground almonds and a little condense milk, served as a pudding – *mousse de gofio*. Wholefood fans also love it as the cereal's husk and seeds are also ground, making *gofio* exceptionally rich in fibre, minerals and vitamins B1 and B2.

Influences from Mainland Spain

Fuerteventura has been Spanish for more than 600 years. This is obviously also reflected in its cuisine. Just as on the mainland, local fare uses lots of olive oil, too. Strolling past the string of restaurants in Morro Jable, for example, you won't be able to miss noticing the smell of garlic in the air either.

meals and are eaten, standing, at the bar. They are normally ready prepared and presented in a glass cabinet on the bar itself – you just have to point to what you want and say '*una ración de este por favor*'. Tapas can equally well be octopus salads or meatballs in a sauce, sardines in vinegar or a slice of *tortilla*.

Tasty tapas, always freshly prepared, are a popular snack among locals, too, as a little something between meals.

Tapas bars, as can be found in virtually every village on Fuerteventura, are a typically Spanish institution. Air-dried ham hanging from the ceiling is often the sign of a well-frequented bar. Cut into wafer-thin slithers, *jamón serrano is served with* manchego cheese or Fuerteventura's own goat's cheese. Tapas are basically bite-sized snacks for in-between

The *tortilla española* is a classic in the Spanish cuisine that, unlike the French variation (*tortilla francesa*), is always made with potatoes and eggs and arrives at the table as a 5cm (2in.)-thick omelette.

Paella, another national dish of Spain, has also made the leap from the mainland to the islands. However, on the Canaries, visitors should be careful – what is served is not seldom anything other than a frozen, pre-prepared meal that is simply heated up in the microwave. Freshly made *paella* is time-consuming and complex. In good restaurants, this rice dish, coloured with saffron and served with seafood, is often only available for two or more people.

Arepas, Empanadas & Co.

Through emigration to Latin America, close ties were forged between the Canary Islands and goat's cheese, crisply cooked and served as a snack – is offered in many Canarian bars. *Empanadas* (a tyepe of filled pasty) originating from Argentina can be found in many places, too. The dish with the strangest name is certainly *ropa vieja* – 'old clothes' – that was traditionally a meal made with the leftovers from the day before. With the addition of fresh ingredients it developed into a much appreciated kind of stew in Cuba and other Latin American countries. While abroad, 'old clothes' is generally

Often spoilt for choice: freshly caught fish are sold and served just where they are brought to land – enjoy!

the continent the other side of the Altlantic. This is also reflected in the local cuisine. The Venezuelan *arepa* – a maize-flour patty filled with either meat or vegetables and made with braised beef and black beans, chickpeas are a basic ingredient in the Canarian version. These are also used for the hearty stew *sopa de garbanzos*.

Julian Diaz shows off some of the goat's cheese in his shop in Tiscamanita.

Say Cheese!

You will come across goats at every turn in the more rural and mountainous areas of Fuerteventura. They provide the milk for the island's only agricultural product of note – Fuerteventura's goat's cheese, that also enjoys a good reputation beyond its own shores.

Queso majorero, named after Fuerteventura's local inhabitants, is available in virtually every supermarket. However, you are better off sampling and buying it directly at a farm cheesemaker's. Surplus production is sent to the neighbouring islands and the Spanish mainland and, with a little bit of luck, it can even be found in specialist shops in other parts of Europe. Whenever the award for the world's best goat's cheese is given every year at one of the international specialist fairs, cheese from Fuerteventura is bound to be up among the winners. To show the importance of cheese to the island, a museum on the subject has been opened on Fuerteventura (p. 82).

Different Varieties

In addition to the non-mature cottage cheese (*queso tierno*), goat's cheese is available at two stages of maturity: from between 21 and 60 days, semi-hard cheese (*semicurado*) and more than two-month old hard cheese (*curado*), similar in consistency to Parmesan and popular among cheese aficionados because of its aromatic flavour. This cheese also has an especially high protein content at 27.5%.

Just like Spanish wines, cheese from Fuerteventura has a *Denominación de Origen Protegida* (*Protected Designation of Origin*) certification that is recognised throughout the EU. Only milk from Majorera goats is used in its production. This breed of dairy goat is especially robust and perfectly adapted to the dry island climate and gives a high-fat milk. Generally, the cheese is made only with goat's milk; it can, however, also be blended with up to a maximum of 15% sheep's milk. A pattern of grooves is typical of the wheels of cheese that can weigh up to 6kg. These marks were originally from the containers made of plaited palmleaves into which the cheese curd was pressed. For reasons of hygiene, these containers are now made of plastic or stainless steel. While a young cheese is almost snow-white, it gains an ivory colour during the maturing process.

Market leader is the Queso Maxorata company in Tuineje that operates a large cheese factory on the road to Gran Tarajal with its own sales outlet. It sells its pasteurised cheese under the names Maxorata, El Tofio and El Pastor Isleño. There are another 23 cheese factories on the island, such as the ones in Antigua, Villaverde and Betancuria. Some also produce unpasteurised cheese, too. The cheese on Fuerteventura is generally not smoked unlike that made on one of the other Canary Islands, La Palma, for example, which is renowned for its mild smoked goat's cheese.

Fuerteventura cheese in its purest form is the *al natural* variety; *al pimentón* has a paprika powder rind and *al gofio* one of *gofio* flour. Curd cheese is served with olives in bars in the form of tapas; in restaurants it is often grilled and coated with a green *mojo* sauce. It can also be eaten as a dessert, sweetened with honey or served with fig purée. So there are lots of different ways for you to enjoy this native produce.

Where the Wild Things Are

Fuerteventura may not have a great choice of indigenous animals but there are three local creatures that almost every visitor will meet!

If Fuerteventura has a national animal it is the goat *(cabra)*. These hardy creatures can scavenge a meal from the meanest terrain, from thorny bushes in rocky outcrops to scrubby foliage among the sand dunes. They total around 60,000 strong, almost as many as the island's resident human population. Goats have been herded since Guanche times and at one time or another most parts of this creature have been put to some practical use. Goat meat and cheese feature prominently on all local restaurant menus, their skins were once used for clothing and their stomachs were used for bags in which *gofio* (p. 29) was stored.

In total there are more than 30 different types of goats on the island. These range from the plain *blanca* (white) and *negro* (black) varieties to the dapple-coated *puipana colorada*, and from cute little kids to huge horned beasts. The hill countryside around Betancuria (p. 70) is a good place to check them out.

Camels

The camel, or rather the single-humped dromedary, was introduced to the island in 1405 by the Spaniards and, being the most efficient creature in this harsh dry terrain, was used in the fields and as a beast of burden right up until the 1950s. In the 16th century there were 4,000 camels on Fuerteventura, but by 1985 there were less than 30. Nowadays, thanks to tourism and the breeding scheme at Oasis Park (p. 113), numbers have recovered to around 300 and Oasis Park has plans to set up the first camel milk dairy in Europe. Camel milk has as much protein but 40 per cent less cholesterol than cow's milk and a high mineral and vitamin C content.

Barbary Ground Squirrels

Erroneously described as chipmunks, these cute little critters

Camels can be found all over the place on Fuerteventura.

Countless little ground squirrels populate the island.

look like a cross between a chipmunk and a grey squirrel and can be seen scuttling almost anywhere on the island where food is being handed out, be it on the promenade in Morro Jable or at the *miradores* of the interior. They are good fun and very tame but it's really not a good idea to feed them as, among other things, this interferes with their natural food-gathering instincts.

Life in the Seas

The climate, clear volcanic sea beds
and depths of up to 3,500m (11,500ft)
make the Canarian archipelago ideal for
diving and deep-sea fishing.

Snorkelling with diving goggles and fins is great
fun for children of all ages.

There is an enormous variety of fish to be caught, including rays, sharks, swordfish, albacora, big-eye, yellow fin and skipjack tuna, bonito, barracuda, wahoo, and the most prestigious and feistiest prize of all, blue marlin. No previous experience is required. All catches belong to the skipper, though most big-game fish are tagged and released. A day's deep-sea fishing, which usually lasts around six hours, costs around €50 per person and there are operators on the quaysides at Caleta de Fuste, Corralejo and Morro Jable.

Whale and Dolphin Spotting
While you may be able to catch sight of whales, dolphins, flying fish and turtles on any sea voyage from Fuerteventura, there are two trips dedicated to spotting these creatures. Boat trips are available both from the harbour in Corralejo and from Morro Jable. The latter is where the catamaran *Santa Maria* is based with which you can go on half-day sailing trips (www. catamaran-santamaria.com/en/), stopping for breaks to swim and snorkel. Food and drinks are of course available on board.

Diving
All operators offer beginner's courses and cater for experienced divers. Angel sharks and rays are the top sights. Recommended operators are Corralejo Dive Centre

(tel: 928 535 906; www.divecentre corralejo.com) and Punta Amanay Dive Centre (tel: 928 535 357; www. punta-amanay.com). The Corralejo Dive Centre is the longest-established on the island, with more than 30 dive sites. A good diving base on the east coast is Deep Blue (tel: 928 163 712; www.deep-blue-diving.com/en/) in Caleta de Fuste; another is Acuarios Jandía (tel: 928 getwet-snorkelling-fuerteventura. com, tel: 660 77 80 53). On these excursions there is a good chance you will spot dolphins, turtles and rays. After a fun high-speed boat ride to the dive site in an inflatable, you don a wetsuit and follow a guide to places where marine life is regularly sighted. Get Wet visits Isla de Lobos. Trips last between two and four hours in total with

Snorkelling safaris and diving trips promise an unforgettable experience in the underwater world.

876 069; www.acuarios-jandia.com), which is based in Costa Calma in the Sotavento Beach Club.

The minimum age for diving is usually 10 or 12 years old.

Snorkelling safaris
You can go on a 'snorkelling safari' with Get Wet in Corralejo (www.

around an hour actually snorkelling. Children over 8 years of age can also take part in snorkel safaris.

Glass bottom boats, which give you an initial impression of the fascinating undersea world, depart from Corralejo harbour to the Isla de Lobos (p. 48).

Evening in Corralejo harbour where fishing boats
and yachts lie at anchor.

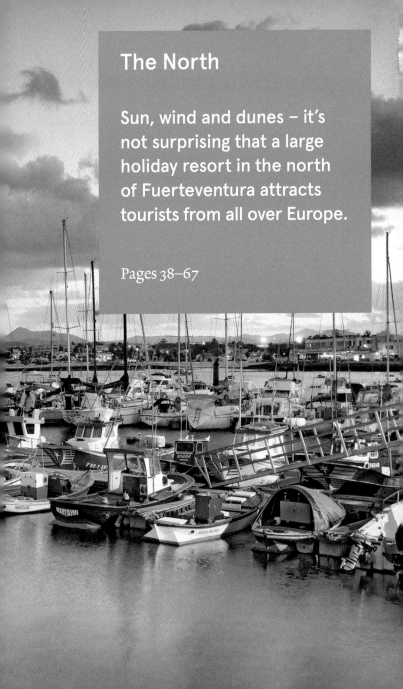

The North

Sun, wind and dunes – it's not surprising that a large holiday resort in the north of Fuerteventura attracts tourists from all over Europe.

Pages 38–67

Getting Your Bearings

Fuerteventura is often described as 'a chip off the Sahara', with the coast of Africa just 100km (60mi) north west of Corralejo. And as you gaze out over the blinding dunes of Corralejo it seems a very apt description. Drive a little way inland and soft white sands change to jagged black rocks – *malpais* (volcanic debris) spilled from the dozens of volcanoes that were active here as recently as 8,000 years ago.

The island's only waymarked trail takes you on a lonely walk right into the heart of these 'badlands', yet the north is also the busiest part of the island. All things are relative of course, and the biggest resort on Fuerteventura would hardly register a blip in Tenerife or Gran Canaria. However, if you have come to the island for peace and quiet, Corralejo should not be your first choice. It has wonderful beaches, a tremendous choice of places to eat, drink and make merry but while the old part retains its fishing village atmosphere, the new 'strip' is modern and noisy.

For a taste of desert island bliss, slip quietly over to the Isla de Lobos. The unspoiled villages of Lajares and Villaverde are perfect country retreats and El Cotillo, with wonderful beaches for all activities and

ages, has a rustic, half-forgotten air, though major new developments may change all that. La Oliva is a quiet community with some intriguing historical and art attractions, while to the south Montaña Tindaya, the sacred mountain of the Guanches, provides a taster of the island's inland delights.

TOP 10
- ❹ ★★ Isla de Lobos
- ❺ ★★ Corralejo
- ❻ ★★ La Oliva

At Your Leisure
- ⓫ El Cotillo
- ⓬ Lajares
- ⓭ Villaverde
- ⓮ Montaña de Tindaya

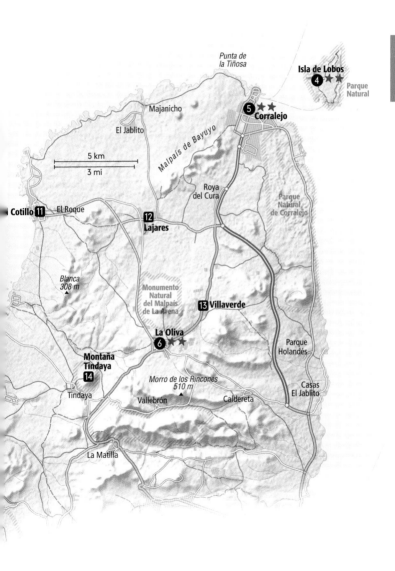

Punta de
la Tiñosa

Isla de Lobos
4 ★ ★
Parque
Natural

Majanicho

5 ★ ★
Corralejo

El Jablito

5 km

3 mi

Roya
del Cura

Malpaís de Bayuyo

Parque
Natural
de Corralejo

Cotillo 11   El Roque

12
Lajares

Blanca
308 m
▲

Monumento
Natural
del Malpaís
de La Arena

13 Villaverde

La Oliva
6 ★ ★

Parque
Holandés

Montaña
Tindaya
14

Morro de los Rincones
510 m
▲

Casas
El Jablito

Tindaya

Vallebrón   Caldereta

La Matilla

My Day
on a Bike in the Northwest Corner of the Island

The stretch of coastline between El Cotillo and Corralejo is not entirely off the tourist track. Nevertheless, if you want to see a bit of unspoilt Fuerteventura, then this is the right place for you. You are best off hiring a bike in El Cotillo. A fresh breeze from the sea will keep you cool all the time but you can always stop at one of several good spots for swimming en route as well.

🕐 10am: Setting off for Surfers' Paradise

With the sea behind you, a new cycle path near the road provides a quick link from the holiday resort **11** El Cotillo to Lajares. The long drawn-out village along the road was once well-known for its delicately hand-crafted products. The *artesanía* on the main road still sells cloth items and hemstitched table sets. The crowds of largely young people, however, that fill the cafés at breakfast time, have little interest in such things. **12** Lajares, where the rent for a holiday flat is still relatively affordable, is popular as it is not far from a number of excellent surfing spots.

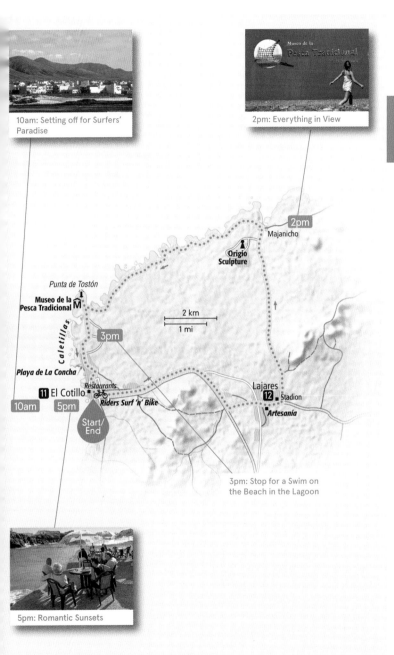

10am: Setting off for Surfers' Paradise

2pm: Everything in View

Museo de la Pesca Tradicional

Punta de Tostón

Museo de la Pesca Tradicional M

Caletillas

3pm

Playa de La Concha

Origio Sculpture

Majanicho 2pm

2 km
1 mi

10am 5pm

11 El Cotillo

Restaurants

Riders Surf 'n' Bike

Start/End

Lajares

12 Stadion

Artesanía

3pm: Stop for a Swim on the Beach in the Lagoon

5pm: Romantic Sunsets

Top: Cycling through the barren volcanic landscape. Above: Fishing on the lava coastline

A remarkable infrastructure has evolved here to serve the surfing scene. Surf shops run by professionals sell made-to-measure boards, small boutiques are well stocked with summery beachwear and organic food shops keep the surfers supplied with all things healthy. If you fancy a smoothie or a genuinely vegan burger then you will find what you want in one of the bistros on the main road. And perhaps one or other craft studio will also be open where you can hunt for a locally made souvenir.

 Noon: In the Middle of Nowhere on the Jagged Lava Coastline

Carry on down the main road as far as the football stadium in Lajares and turn off towards Majanicho. Without

Left, top and centre: Fashion boutiques in Lajares. Left, bottom: Holiday complex with Origo Mare sculpture in Majanicho. Above: Faro de Tostón lighthouse

any gradients worth mentioning, you cycle on towards the sea again through a barren landscape with volcanoes dotted about and a few un-demanding plants that hardly merit the term 'vegetation'. The surround-ing area is so austere that it somehow has an appeal of its very own.

Majanicho, a narrow bay with a couple of dozen cube-like houses around a dark pebbly beach, still looks the way many places on the coast of Fuerteventura once did some 25 years ago. Apart from a surf club on the sand, tourism here has not found a foothold. The collection of bungalows a little further inland is mostly rented by individualists who are interested neither in a wide promenade nor in a spectacular beach just outside the door.

An artistic accent is seet by the huge sculpture in Origo Mare, made of welded brass sections, that is visible from a long way away. As large as an elephant it stands out in the flat sur-roundings and is not totally unlike an elephant in appearance either.

3pm

The turquoise-coloured water in the crescent-shaped Playa de la Concha is especially calm and clear.

2pm: Everything in View

In Majanicho take the track that runs parallel to the sea heading westwards. You may have to push your bike a few yards in some places where the track is just sand. The light-coloured sand provides a stark contrast to the dark, volcanic coastline. A few camper vans are usually parked in the middle of nowhere and, out at sea, skilled surfers wait for the ultimate wave. Three lighthouses welcome visitors to the Punta de Tostón in the far northwestern corner of the island. The smallest of them was built in 1897 to help ships navigate the straits safely between Fuerteventura and Lanzarote. It later transpired that it was too low, so a second, octagonal lighthouse was built in 1960 and, in 1985, a third one was erected with a 30m (100ft)-high

El Cotillo – delicious food can be enjoyed in the fish restaurants on the old harbour as the sun sets.

tower. The former lighthouse keeper's home is now a fishing museum that reflects the hard life led by the fishermen of old. The viewing platform in the tower is more interesting than the exhibition for most (included in the admission fee).

3pm: Stop for a Swim on the Beach in the Lagoon

Nothing against bumpy tracks, but fortunately things get better after the lighthouses. The road

5pm

heading south is a smooth ride. The turquoise-coloured water and the beaches on <u>Caletillas</u> lagoon in front of you are an open invitation for a swim. Among the most beautiful is the crescent-shaped <u>Playa de la Concha</u> (shell bay). Protected by a natural reef a quick break here for a dip is an absolute must. The fine, light-coloured sand and the gentle slope into the water add to the overall enjoyment – swimming at its best!

5pm: Romantic Sunsets

End your short cycling trip at the old harbour in <u>El Cotillo</u>. The fishing boats have long since moved to the new harbour, leaving a handful of fish restaurants behind together with a dreamy view over the harbour bay. This is where you can pick what is, without doubt, one of the ultimate spots when the sun goes down. And the fish on the hot stone tastes takes some beating, too.

❹ ★★ Isla de Lobos

Why	A peaceful contrast to the bustling holiday resorts.
Don't Miss	Hiking and relaxing on an uninhabited island.
Time	One whole day.
What Else	Botanists will find the vaste amounts of spurge interesting.
In Short	Not only one but three islands can be seen from the top of the Montaña de la Caldera.

It seems everything on the Isla de Lobos qualifies itself by a diminutive; *las lagunitas*, the little lagoons; *los hornitos*, the little volcanoes; El Puertito, the (ramshackle) little port. We would add to that by saying that this is the best little day trip that you can make. The absence of tourist development means that you can see an almost pristine island in its original state.

The island in the straits between Fuerteventura and Lanzarote covers an area of just 4.4km² (1.7mi²) – and you can walk right round this uninhabited and car-free island in three hours. The island's name, literally 'island of wolves', is derived from a colony of monk seals *(lobo marino)* that once lived here but have long since died out. It is recorded that the conquistador Gadifer de la Salle (number two to Jean de Béthencourt, p. 18) dropped anchor here in 1402 and he and his men were only saved from starving by eating seal meat. Béthencourt built a hermitage on the island and in the following centuries Lobos was used as a pirate and slave-trading base. Today, António, the ex-lighthouse keeper, now island restaurateur, his family and a few friends inhabit the dilapidated little hamlet of El Puertito in season. The lighthouse still functions but is now fully automated.

Getting Here
The short crossing to the island is an experience in itself. A small ferry departs from the harbour in Corralejo for the 20-minute journey to the neighbouring island and provides a wonderful view of the north coast of Fuerteventura. If you want to hike around Lobos, take the first ferry that

View of the island volcano from Playa de la Caleta.

leaves at 10am. That will give you enough time to see everything on the island as well a relaxing swim before taking the last boat back to the Playa de la Concha at around 4pm. A delightful bay, perfect for a swim, is just a few minutes walk from where the boat comes in. Make sure you take lots of drinking water with you as well as something to eat. There is only one (very modest) place that serves food which, in addition, has to be ordered in advance during the crossing.

Getting About

A visitor centre *(centro de visitantes)*, located where the boat comes in, gives some information about the fauna and flora on the island that is a designated nature park. The low wooden building, the only proper building as such on the island, is the starting point of the waymarked path around the island. It you turn right, you will reach Puertito in about seven minutes – a simple collection of shack-like structures where the fishermen store their equipment. The island's only eatery is housed in one of these huts. Following the path up the east side of the little island, heading northwards, you will reach the Faro de

Two boats run to Isla de Lobos, including a glass-bottomed catamaran

Martiño after about an hour from where you can enjoy the wonderful view towards Lanzarote from the hill with the lighthouse.

If you take the path to the left of the visitor centre, the Playa de la Concha with its fine sand is reached after about ten minutes. This is where many people spend the whole day before catching the return boat.

Good views can be enjoyed from the summit of the only larger volcano on the island, the Montaña de la Caldera (127m/417ft) that is right in front of you. The climb is not particularly difficult but you do need good shoes and have to be sure-footed. The path from the Playa de la Concha cannot be missed. The climb to the marker post at the top on the rim of the crater takes a good half-an-hour.

INSIDER TIP If you intend to eat at the island restaurant you MUST order on the ferry.

 ✝ 191 E5

Centro des Visitantes Isla de Lobos
✉ Muelle ⏲ Daily 10:30–3

❺ ★★ Corralejo

Why	The largest seaside resort in the north of Fuerteventura.
Don't Miss	The desert-like sand dunes.
Time	Two to three hours.
What Else	There are some good places to eat on the promenade with harbour views.
In Short	You will feel you have saved yourself a trip to the Sahara!

The biggest resort on the island, Corralejo, has a loyal following, particularly among British and German visitors. The town divides neatly into the 'old port' and the 'new resort', the dividing line being the pedestrianised zone. Just beyond this is the original fishing harbour, now a busy port where the Lanzarote and Lobos ferries, big-game fishing yachts and sleek catamarans jostle for space alongside traditional fishing boats.

The old part of town, particularly around the pedestrianised zone, is a picturesque area of small alleys and squares, most of which lead onto the seafront promenade which is lined with attractive restaurants and bars. The epicentre of nocturnal activities is 'Music Square', a tiny quadrangle hemmed in by restaurants with waiters touting for trade and a small stage where musicians serenade diners. To find the most authentic

Corralejo is one of the largest tourist centres on the island, as is reflected in the wide choice of restaurants and bars.

There are plenty of interesting sights, including the modern architecture

Spanish and local bars and restaurants, and some quaint little shops, just go a block or two further on towards the port. On Calle La Ballena it's hard to go wrong.

The modern part of town lies to either side of the Avenida Nuestra Señora del Carmen, also called the 'The Strip'. The Avenida is not unattractive and has several shopping centres, but don't expect to buy designer clothes here. This is primarily where you can find surfing gear and summery beachwear. Large apartment complexes adjoin the Avenida and offer a huge range of restaurants and bars. A visit to one of the eateries on the Avenida Marítima, the car-free promenade that runs southwards from the harbour, however, is more appealing. You can watch the car-ferries coming in and departing from and to Lanzarote. One or the other old fishing boat can be found among the modern yachts.

Corralejo has no classic tourist attractions as such. The Acua Water Park (formerly Baku) is well-visited on hot summer days. Covering an area of 2.5 ha (6 acres), it was first opened in 2004 but is now showing its age in parts. Nevertheless, children will love the mega-slide and the wave pool. A large market (mercadillo) is held every Friday morning which also sells clothes and a few handicrafts. Many of the products, however, are cheap items for gullible tourits.

Beaches

Basically speaking, everything in Corralejo revolves around the beach. The town harbour beach is the easy option, right in the centre, although it can get crowded. It is also not always as clean as one might wish. Look out for some very artistic and sophisticated sand sculptures here and do throw a coin or two in the artist's hat, particularly if you take a photograph. Moving east from the harbour a narrow beach runs almost all the way along the front. Playa Galera, in front of the Corralejo Beach hotel, is a nice stretch.

Locals outside the fish restaurant Cofradia de Pescadores

The best beaches lie 500m or so east of here and stretch for around 7km (4mi). You can easily walk from the newer part of town.

Flag Beach is the main section and the next stretch along, by the two large Riu hotels, is known as Glass Beach. Windsurfers and kiteboarders will head to Flag Beach or Glass Beach but there are excellent surfing 'beaches' (with no sand) heading west from the Bristol Playas apartments.

Camel trail in the dunes near Corralejo

Whichever beach you choose, directly across the water you will enjoy great views of Isla de Lobos and Lanzarote.

Parque Natural de las Dunas de Corralejo

Corralejo's white sand dunes cover around 27km² (10mi²). This area was declared a national park in 1982, too late to stop the two hotels that had already been built, but it has prevented further attempts to exploit this otherwise pristine natural landscape.

Bulldozers occasionally have to clear the road here from sand drifts to make it passable again. But a few yards to the side you can walk along the sand – barefoot of course – to your heart's content and stroll across the dunes. Just a few undemanding species of plant survive in the valleys between the ridges of sand, such as sea spurge (*Euphorbia paralias*) and 'uva de mar' – sea grape – (*Tetraena fontanesii*)

INSIDER TIP Front row seats: In **Antiguo Café del Puerto** (p. 63) you can enjoy your tapas right on the harbourside.

 ✝ 191 E5

Acua Water Park
✉ Avenida Nuestra Señora del Carmen

☎ 928 867 227
🌐 www.acuawaterpark.com
🕐 Daily April–early Nov 10–5 (later in season) 🎟 €25

❻ ★★ La Oliva

Why	Surprising discoveries in the peaceful interior.
Don't Miss	Relics from the colonial past.
Time	Two hours.
What Else	Genuine old Canarian art can be found in the Centro de Arte Canario.
In Short	A former capital that is little more than a largish village.

Despite being the administrative centre of the north, La Oliva is no more than a large village and often has the appearance of a ghost town. Nonetheless, it has an interesting history and a number of unusual sights.

La Oliva has always been a seat of power on Fuerteventura. The Guanche king Guize (p. 14) once ruled his northern territory from here and, after the conquest, it was one of the first towns to be settled by the Europeans.

The Iglesia de Nuestra Señora de la Candelaria, built in 1711, has three naves, but its most striking feature is its black lava bell tower. Look inside to see its wine-glass-shaped

View of the courtyard of Casa de los Coroneles in Oliva

The Casa de los Coroneles with its ornate shutters.

pulpit and side altar decorated in matching patterns and its painting of Christ in Majesty (1732).

Casa de los Coroneles

In the 18th century, La Oliva was the seat of the military governor *(Los Coroneles)* and at times the de facto capital of Fuerteventura. These ruthless commanders ruled here until 1859, their official residence was the grandiose Casa de los Coroneles, a large castellated colonial-style house dating back to 1650. It is now one of the most historically interesting buildings on the island. It used to be said, quite erroneously, that there was a door and window for every day of the year and it is thought that the saying probably reflected the jealous unpopularity of the Colonel's regime. This came to an end in 1859 and thereafter the famous old house began a long slow decline into dereliction. Today, Casa de Coroneles is an art gallery and cultural centre (www.lacasadeloscoroneles.org; Tue–Sat 10–6; €3).

Centro de Arte Canario (CAC) – Casa Mané

This cool contemporary space devoted to Canarian art, complete with soothing ambient New Age music, has wide-ranging appeal. The entrance is via a <u>cactus garden</u> with interesting sculptures well-worth a closer look.

The 72 metal cut-outs that make up the 'Herd of Goats' by the Catalan artist Albert Argulló, cannot be missed. He sees his work as a homage to what is by far the most important working animal on Fuerteventura. A ramp, almost 100m (328ft) long, leads to the subterranean exhibition room where works largely by Canarian artists are on show, including Octavio del Toro from Gran Canaria and César Manrique from Lanzarote.

Museo del Grano La Cilla

The small but interesting Grain Museum is housed is a former granary (*cilla* – lit. silo) dating from 1819. In days of old, tithes in the form of produce paid by farmers to the church were stored here. In addition to historical photographs of farming, ploughs and camel muzzles are on display. The building itself is interesting with an old terracotta floor and lime plastered walls as once found all over the island.

Art treasures in the Centro de Arte Canario

The Casa del Capellán, south of the parish church, still awaits renovation. The masonry work around the door and the windows of the old chaplain's house appear to have been executed by the same craftsman who created the Aztec patterns on the church portal in Pájara (p. 78).

INSIDER TIP La Oliva is short of good cafés or restaurants but try **Kiosco La Oliva** opposite the church.

✛ 191 D3

ⓘ

Centro de Arte Canario (CAC) – Casa Mané
✉ Calle Salvador Manrique de Lara (opposite Casa de los Coroneles)
☎ 928 851 128
🌐 www.centrodeartecanario.com
🕐 Mon–Sat 10–5 💶 €4

Museo del Grano La Cilla
✉ Carretera El Cotillo
☎ 928 868 728
🕐 Tue 10–3, 4–6, Fri 10–3, Sat 10–2
💶 €1.50

Fisherman monument in the old harbour of El Cotillo

At Your Leisure

11 El Cotillo

Compared to its larger neighbour Corralejo, tourism in this old fishing village on the northwest coast of Fuerteventura is less obtrusive. Although a number of new holiday flats have been built in the past few years, people come here more for the peace and quiet it offers. The area around the Puerto Viejo (old harbour) is especially attractive. There are several good fish restaurants (p. 64) here which also attract day-tourists from elsewhere. One of the village's landmarks is the Torre del Tostón. Built in 1743 as a defense tower to scare British and Moorish pirates away, it now houses the tourist information office. During opening hours you can go onto the roof of the round building and look over Puerto Nuevo to the new harbour where colourful fishing boats bob about in a bay protected by rocks. The almost 6m (20ft)-long skeleton of a beaked whale – probably killed during a navy manoeuvre – stands in front of the tower. Two conical kilns to one side of the Torre del Tostón are a reminder of the lime-burners who worked here well into the 20th century.

Just south of the El Cotillo is the Playa del Castillo, one of Fuerteventura's most beautiful beaches. However, the big waves make it better for surfing than swimming. The Playa de los Lagos to the north is better for families.

✛ 190 C4

Torre del Tostón
🕐 Mon–Fri 10–3, Sat, Sun 10–2
💶 €1.50

12 Lajares

Although it isn't on the sea, this long drawn-out village along the road between Corralejo and El Cotillo is a popular meeting place for the surfing crowd as there are lots of trendy pubs and craft studios here in addition to shops selling surfing equipment. Lajares is also known for its long-established School of Embroidery, nowadays incorporated into an *artesanía* (handicrafts) shop (p. 66). There

Lajares is famous for its school of embroidery.

are two fine examples of restored windmills near the church to the south of Lajares and the village is also the starting point for the Sendero de Bayuyo footpath (p. 164).

✛ 191 D4

13 Villaverde

Villaverde is one of the best-preserved villages on the island. Perhaps the villagers are following the lead of the exemplary Hotel Rural Mahoh (p. 62), which stands at the southern end of Villaverde and is worth a visit for its architecture and sculpture garden alone. The equally neat and tidy black-and-white stone farm buildings of La Rosita mark the northern entrance to the village. In the 1920s this was a tobacco and maize farm. A cactus garden surrounds the residence used until recently as an agricultural museum.

From La Rosita head towards the centre of Villaverde and take the first turn right; after 300m is the Cueva del Llanos. This cave is actually part of a much larger lava tube formed more than 690,000 years ago. The entrance to the cave is a part of the tube where the roof has collapsed (known as a *jameo*) and contains a visitor centre with an exhibition, café and shop. From here visitors can walk along a lit pathway 400m into the cave which is some 7–10m (23–32ft) wide.

In 2018, the cave was closed because of flooding, so enquire when you get to Villaverde whether it is now possible to go inside again.

✝ 191 D3

14 Montaña de Tindaya

The original island dwellers regarded this mountain as sacred and came up here to worship their Supreme Deity, offering young goats as sacrifices. Their legacy is a number of inscriptions and rock carvings, only discovered as recently as 1978, on and around the summit of the mountain at about 400m (1,300ft).

Climbing the mountain is now forbidden in order to protect it as a natural monument and to prevent the rock engravings from being vandalised. Montaña Tindaya became internationally known through the sculptor Eduardo Chillida (1924–2002) who wanted

to hollow out the mountain to create a 'Monument to Emptiness and Tolerance'. Even after the artist's death, the feasibility (and especially the financing) of this ambitious proejct were discussed for several years. In the meantime it has now been put on hold.

Tindaya itself is a small agricultural community that lives primarily from goat farming. Apart from the little parish church, a visit to the Casa Alta de Tindaya on the western edge of the village is worthwhile. This large country home from the 18th century, surrounded by a crenellated wall, has been beautifully and comprehensibly restored. It is intended to house a museum on the history of Montaña Tindaya.

To the east of Tindaya a narrow lane leads to the hamlet of Vallebrón. At the half-way point, a short detour to the Mirador Montaña de la Muda can be recommended from where you have a wonderful view of Montaña Tindaya. The little village of Vallebrón lies at the foot of the range of mountains that rises to a height of 500m (1640ft). As a consequence, it has a comparatively high rainfall and, in spring, the terraced fields are really green. Inside the small Ermita de San Pedro y San Juan (18th century) is a colourful Baroque altarpiece.

Restored farmhouse: La Rosita

✝ 190 C3

Fuerte's Holy Mountain

Montaña de Tindaya was considered holy by the
first inhabitants of the Canary Islands. Among
other figures, they left enigmatic silhouettes
of human feet engraved in the stone near the
summit. The sculptor Eduardo Chillida even
wanted to hollow ouf a 'Monument to Emptiness
and Tolerance' under the pyramid-shaped mountain. It's a great shame that it can no longer be
climbed. But even from a distance the towering
chunk of trachyte casts its mysterious spell –
especially at dusk when the sun bathes its flanks
a deep red.

Where to... Stay

Expect to pay per double room, per night
€ under €60
€€ €60–€90
€€€ €91–€120
€€€€ over €120

Note that many of the larger hotels and apartments in Corralejo are block booked by big tour operators.

CORRALEJO

Atlantis Bahía Real €€€€
If your idea of a holiday is pampered luxury, then this 5-star 250-room grand hotel in Moorish-style right on the beachfront, just out of town, is ideal. All rooms enjoy magnificent sea views, there are three gourmet restaurants to eat your way through and the largest and best-equipped spa on the island, with a Turkish Bath, an ice fountain, a shower temple, a large open-air jacuzzi, a spinning room and just about any treatment you could wish for.
🕂 191 E5 ✉ Avenida Grandes Playas s/n
☎ 928 537 153
🌐 www.atlantisbahiareal.com

Corralejo Beach €
One of the town's oldest accommodations, the Corralejo Beach enjoys a good beachfront location right in the centre of the resort. It includes 156 studios and apartments, with basic but functional furnishings, many with views towards Lanzarote and Isla de Lobos.
🕂 191 E5 ✉ Calle Víctor Gra Bassas 1
☎ 928 535 651
🌐 www.corralejobeach.com

Avanti €€€€
Since 1969 this boutique hotel has been one of the best places to stay in the former fishing village. Recently completely revamped, its location right on the sandy beach is hard to beat. From the jacuzzi on the roof terrace you have a wonderful view of the island of Lobos. Adults only.
🕂 191 E5 ✉ Calle Delfín 1 ☎ 928 867 523
🌐 www.avantihotelboutique.com

Hesperia Bristol Playa €€
This attractive 3-keys aparthotel is situated on the seafront near the port and comprises 186 units in landscaped gardens. Apartments are well equipped and have a kitchen; facilities include three swimming pools, a gym and a pleasant bar in the garden to while away the time.
🕂 191 E5
✉ Urbanización Lago de Bristol 1
☎ 928 867 020
🌐 www.nh-hotels.com

The pool and beach at Riu Palace Tres Islas

Riu Palace Tres Islas €€€€
Architecturally speaking, this six-storeyed building from the 1970s is not particularly appealing. This 4-star hotel stands out all the more thanks to its situation on the edge of the magnificent dunes. Both the dunes and the beach are just a hop, skip and jump away. The Riu La Oliva, under the same management, is located next to it. These are the only hotels far and wide in this area that was later made a nature reserve.
🕂 191 E5
✉ Avenida Grandes Playas
☎ 928 535 700 🌐 www.riu.com

VILLAVERDE

Hotel Rural Mahoh €€
The Mahoh is an old country house built from volcanic stone and wood and dates from the 19th century. It has nine bedrooms with stone floors, all furnished with antiques, four of them with four-poster beds, and all exuding a rustic and romantic feel. Within its manicured grounds there is a swimming pool, a multi-purpose sports area with

tennis and horse-riding stables. Its restaurant is one of the best on the island so *media pensión* (half board) is recommended. Breakfast is included in the price.

✈ 191 D3 ✉ Sitio de Juan Bello, Carretera Villaverde–La Oliva
☎ 928 868 050 ⊕ www.mahoh.com

EL COTILLO

Casa Tile €€
Set 2km (1mi) inland from El Cotillo this mid-19th-century country house is a perfect holiday hideaway for up to four people. The house has been in the same family for more than 150 years and has been sympathetically renovated and restored. The living area, bath-room and bedrooms are separated from the kitchen and dining area by an open court-yard and there is a small pool. Other facilities include a TV, washing machine and barbecue.

✈ 190 C4
✉ El Roque ☎ 928 851 620
⊕ www.momentorural.com/en/

Cotillo Sunset Apartments €–€€
Right on the beach and a five-minute walk from the beautiful Lagos coves, this smart modern complex comprises 32 two-storey studios. Each is attractively furnished and have well-equipped kitchens, including a microwave oven and toaster. All have a balcony/terrace with patio furniture. There is a pool and a heated outdoor jacuzzi.

✈ 190 C4
✉ Avenida de los Dos Lagos
☎ 928 175 065

LAJARES

El Patio de Lajares €€€
This charming, stylish German-run guest-house is entered via a patio and has six com-fortable and spacious air-conditioned rooms. Each has a terrace, satellite TV (English channels), mini bar, and a luxurious bathroom. There's a swimming pool, and wellness facili-ties include a Japanese foot bath, a small fitness centre and aloe vera treatments.

✈ 191 D4
✉ Calle la Cerca 9, Lajares
☎ 650 134 030 ⊕ www.patio-lajares.com

Where to... Eat and Drink

Expect to pay for a meal for one, excluding drinks
€   under €15
€€   €15–€25
€€€   over €25

CORRALEJO

La Scarpetta da Mario €€–€€€
There may be no sea view from this Italian restaurant but Scarpetta da Mario in the Plaza Shopping Center serves good home-made pasta and pizzas. Fish and seafood dishes are prepared on a stone grill.

✈ 191 E5
✉ Avenida Señora del Carmen 62
☎ 928 535 887 ⊕ www.scarpetamario.com
⏰ Daily 1:30–11:30

Antiguo Café del Puerto €€
This is the sort of place you will be welcome at any time of day or night, whether you want a *café con leche* or a beer while watching the boats on the seafront, or to make up a meal from the good choice of tasty tapas.

✈ 191 E5
✉ Calle La Ballena ☎ 928 537 024
⏰ Thu–Tue 11am–1am

Caracoles €€
Sylvia and Carlos are well known to Corralejo regulars for their authentic Spanish/Canarian cooking and serving up some of the best tapas to be found in town. An attractive little bar set in a narrow alleyway just off Music Square, it is unlikely to disappoint. Special offers such as six tapas and a bottle of wine for a set price makes the choosing less of a chore for confused visitors who would like a taste of everything.

✈ 191 E5
✉ Just off Music Square
⏰ Tue–Sun 7–11pm
(closed last Sun of month)

Factoria €–€€
Set right on the seafront, but just away from the main hubbub, this cheerful little pizzeria is one of the friendliest places in Corralejo. They do steaks and fish too but specialise in

pizzas. The view over the water to the island of Lobos is lovely.
⚓ 191 E5
✉ Avenida Marítima ☎ 928 535 726
🕐 Daily 10:30am–11pm

Café Latino €–€€
This café-restaurant on the promenade has a wonderful location on the harbourside. With its wide range of pasta dishes, pizzas and tortillas, it is much more than a mere café as its name would imply. However, you can come here just for a sangria or an Italian Peroni beer if you like and settle down on the large terrace to enjoy the view of the harbour.
⚓ 191 E5
✉ Avenida Marítimo 6 ☎ 606 441 725
🕐 Daily 9–8:30

Taberna Fogalera €–€€
Open in the evenings, this seafront restaurant on the pedestrianised promenade serves Mediterranean cuisine, which besides Italian risotto and pasta also includes a good Spanish paella. Even the selection of wines is from Italy and Spain. There is a special children's menu: *'menù bambini'*.
⚓ 191 E5
✉ Avenida Marítima 12 ☎ 928 867 676
🕐 Wed–Mon 6pm–11pm

EL COTILLO

Aguayre €
This trendy modern bar overlooking the new port is the ideal place to catch the famous El Cotillo sunset with a beer, smoothie, milk-shake or *chai latte* in your hand. Mexican buritos and other international light meals are also served.
⚓ 190 C4
✉ Calle La Caleta 5 ☎ 928 538 745
🕐 Daily 9:30–9

Azzurro €€
In the detached house on the road to Faro del Tostón, the menu includes Italian dishes, a broad range of Canarian dishes and a good choice of vegetarian dishes. The paella and the *scoglio* (seafood) *tagliatelle* with mushrooms and prawns in a parmesan

nest are highly recommended. Relax in the cosy traditional stone interior or on the terrace, watching the sunset alongside a mixed crowd of diners. Azzurro provides excellent service and superb house wines.
⚓ 190 C4
✉ Urb. Los Lagos 1, Carretera al Faro
☎ 928 175 360 🌐 www.azzurro.es
🕐 Tue–Sun 12:30–10:30

El Goloso €
The French bakery on the northern edge of El Cotillo has a tempting selection of baguettes, croissants, country-style breads, various quiches, delicious fruit tartlets and other sweet pastries. You can buy everything to take away, but there are a few small tables for people who want to enjoy their breakfast and a good coffee in the bakery. In the main season, El Goloso is always busy.
⚓ 190 C4 ✉ Calle Pedro Cabrera Saavedra/ Calle León y Castillo ☎ 928 53 86 68
🕐 7:30–2:30, 5–8, Sun in the morning only

Torino €–€€
This friendly little beach bar next to the lagoon beaches serves a good range of snacks and full meals and is the ideal place to eat with warm sand between your toes. The garlic prawns are wonderful and the paella is good, but give the cheese and tomato salad a miss.
⚓ 190 C4
✉ Playa Lagos 🕐 Daily 10–5

La Vaca Azul €€
The 'Blue Cow' on the old harbour is one of the most popular restaurants in the village. The tables on the roof terrace in particular are quickly taken. As in the other restaurants around about, fish is the dish of choice here.
⚓ 190 C4
✉ Muelle Viejo ☎ 928 538 685
🕐 Daily 12:30–11

LAJARES

El Arco €
This pleasant café for the 'in' crowd on the through road is a meeting place from break-fast onwards. Apart from the homemade

burgers, the generously filled *bocadillos* are very popular – both are available for vegetarians as well.

✚ 191 D4 ✉ Carretera General 44 ☎ 928 868 671 🕐 Thu–Wed 12:30–10

Canela €–€€

The plain tables and chairs on the pavement in front of the Canela and inside give this popular café/restaurant an air of no-frills simplicity. Located on the main street of Lajares, it is a favourite haunt of the younger crowd, who go there during the day to enjoy the colourful fusion cuisine of Asian curries, Arab Falafel, Greek salad and Mexican burritos. From 6pm, the kitchen extends its repertoire to include steaks.

✚ 191 D4 ✉ Calle Coronel Gonzalez del Hiero 34 (Main road from Lajares–El Cotillo) ☎ 928 861 712 🕐 Daily 8am–2am

LA OLIVA

Hijos de Suarez €

Considering it is the administrative centre of the north, La Oliva's choice of restaurants is fairly modest. Opposite the parish church, you can buy simple meals, sandwiches *(bocadillos)* and freshly pressed juices and sit at one of the small tables on the pavement to eat them.

✚ 191 D3 ✉ Opposite the Iglesia Nuestra Señora de la Candelaria ☎ 928 868 679 🕐 Daily 10–7

VILLAVERDE

El Horno €€€

The large barbecue at the entrance to this attractive rustic restaurant tells you that the speciality of the house is grilled meats. Apart from steaks, you can also sample typically Canarian dishes here such as rabbit and kid. Finish with fig or *gofio* ice cream.

✚ 191 D3
✉ Carretera General Villaverde–La Oliva, 191 ☎ 928 868 671, 629 382 304 🕐 Mon–Sat 12:30pm–11pm, Sun until 10pm

Hotel Rural Mahoh €€

Choose from one of the most interesting Canarian menus on the island while relaxing

Traditional food is served at Horno.

in one of its most charming settings. Start with delicious home made croquettes, or stuffed peppers; for mains try rabbit, goat ragout or veal, and finish with fig ice cream smothered in mouth-watering warm chocolate sauce.

✚ 191 D3 ✉ Sitio de Juan Bello, Carretera Villaverde–La Oliva ☎ 928 868 050 🌐 www. mahoh.com 🕐 Daily 1–11

TINDAYA

Los Podomorfos €–€€

Named after the silhouettes of human feet on Montaña Tindaya, this eatery serves good vegetarian food in addition to goat's meat burgers. The terrace offers wonderful views of Montaña Tindaya.

✚ 190 C3 ✉ Calle Virgen de la Caridad 70 ☎ 928 865 578 🕐 Wed–Sun 11–7

Where to… Shop

Shopping in the north of the island is concentrated on the *centros comerciales* (shopping centres) and main street of Corralejo. There are very few shops elsewhere in this region.

CORRALEJO

The resort's 'high street', Avenida Nuestra Señora del Carmen, and the many shopping centres that lead off here feature scores of fashion clothes shops. Surf wear is predominant. International retail names sell at similar prices to northern Europe. Anyone looking for original Italian ladies' fashions should go to the Shopping Center Campanario in Las Gatas with its Gaudí-like entrance.

Another unusual shop is the Panadería de Don Juan at number 20. This old-fashioned, long-established bakery is ideal if you're self catering and they have a small café attached, too.

Cool t-Shirts and accessories bearing the goat skeleton logo of Extreme Animals are available in the Calle Las Dunas.

If you are after the ethnic look, Indian jewellery and Thai silver, then rummage through the Isis Boutique – Aladdin's Cave (Calle La Iglesia 3).

The Herbolario Pachamama has a large selection of organic food and natural cosmetics (Calle Francisco Navarro Artiles 2).

Small wooden sheep with woolly fleeces in a shop in Lajares

There are some pleasant little individual outlets dotted around the harbour. Mystic (corner of Calle María Santana Figueroa/ Calle Isla de Lobos) sells souvenirs from around the world as well as natural sponges and aloe vera products.

Corralejo's market (p. 52) takes place every Friday 9am to 1pm at Acua Water Park on Avenida Nuestra Señora del Carmen and is a good place to go if you enjoy African-style goods.

LA OLIVA

The Centro de Arte Canario sells a wide range of works by local artists, from inexpensive postcards to expensive originals.

LAJARES

Lajares is famous for its embroidery school, which is now part of one of the island's best *artesanías* (craft shops). You'll find it on the main road in the centre of the village. Founded in 1950, it claims to be the only original Canarian embroidery workshop on the island and is famous for its openwork embroidery tablecloths and napkins as well as lace items.

The Artesanía Lajares also sells a wide range of other handicrafts, plus aloe vera products, clothing, food, wine, cheese and preserves.

Surfers regularly pass through Lajares en route to neighbouring El Cotillo and there are a handful of specialist surfing shops. If you need a board, suit or just a t-shirt then Witchcraft and North Shore at either end of the village have some funky gear and anything else a surfer may need today.

Where to... Go Out

The beaches of Corralejo and El Cotillo are famous for their excellent water sports conditions (p. 21). Corralejo is also a lively town after dark – the action is largely dispersed among its many disco and karaoke bars, sports bars and British-style pubs, although there are no 'major' nightclubs to speak of.

The glass bottom boat to Los Lobos lets you catch a glimpse of the seabed beneath.

WATER SPORTS

For the best windsurfing and kiteboarding (p. 21), go to the Playas de Corralejo and Playa Castillo at El Cotillo.

Flag Beach Windsurf and Kitesurf Centre (tel: 928 866 389; 630 062 131, UK 0871 711 5036; www.flagbeach.com) is the north's biggest and longest-established water sports operator. It is located on Flag Beach. Windsurfing, kiteboarding and traditional (wave) surfing courses are offered here, for example (tel: 928 866 389; www.flagbeach.com).

NIGHTLIFE

Corralejo bars and pubs play host to a lively music scene. One of the best is the Rock Island Bar (www.rockislandbar.com) at Calle Crucero Baleares, with live acoustic acts every evening.

Another venue for live acts is the Rock Café in Avenida Nuestra Señora del Carmen (in the La Plaza Shopping Center).

Located right on the beach, the Waikiki Beach Club has been one of the most popular clubs for night-owls for years (Avenida Hernández Morán 11; www.waikikibeachclub.es). During the day, it is run as a bistro. In the evenings and at night you can come here to chill out over tropical cocktails and good music. Every evening on the plaza surrounded by terrace cafés in the old town centre, a band plays evergreens and Spanish music.

EXCURSIONS

BY BOAT

Ferries to Lanzarote (p. 128 ff) depart from the harbour in Corralejo several times a day.

There are also small excursion boats that visit Lobos (p. 48). You can also round the island of Lobos on a 4-hour catamaran trip from Flag Beach (www.flagbeach.com) which also gives you enough time for a swim and for snorkelling.

ON LAND

The number one bike centre is Easy Riders in the Calle Las Dunas (tel: 928 867 005; www.easyriders-bikecenter.com/e/). The bike specialist hires out bikes and offers guided day trips catering to different levels of competence.

WALKING

The Sendero de Bayuyo is very impressive, leading from Lajares through a strange volcanic landscape to the Calderón Hondo crater (p. 164).

A huge sculpture of a nautilus in the harbour of Puerto del Rosario

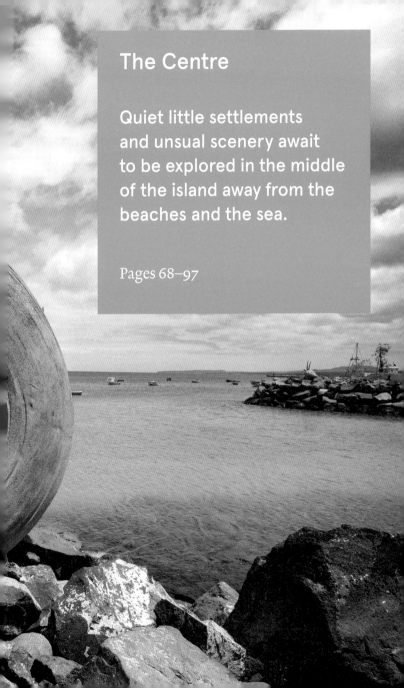

The Centre

Quiet little settlements
and unsual scenery await
to be explored in the middle
of the island away from the
beaches and the sea.

Pages 68–97

Getting Your Bearings

The interior of Fuerteventura is home to spectacular mountain scenery and the villages of Betancuria, Vega de Río Palmas, Pájara and Antigua are the oldest and among the most picturesque on the island. You can trace their history through their beautiful churches and colonial architecture and as a bonus they also have some of the finest places to eat.

The greatest attraction away from the sea is the delightful little old town of Betancuria located in an upland valley. While the former capital of the island is a monument to Fuerteventura's major historical events, the Ecomuseo de La Alcogida at Tefía is the no-less-fascinating story of how ordinary *majoreros* have eked a living from this harsh land in the past. The drive from Tefía via Betancuria to Pájara is along one of the most beautiful stretches of countryside on the island, and there are frequent *miradores* (viewing points) from which to enjoy the ancient landscape. On the east coast the proximity of the airport and the resort of Caleta de Fuste means it's very popular with British holidaymakers. To the north lies the capital of Puerto del Rosario while just south the little fishing hamlet of Salinas del Carmen is worth a visit.

The west coast of Fuerteventura is virtually untouched by tourism. Ajuy, from where you can take a short walk to the Caleta Negra sea cave, is well worth a visit. Due to the continuously surging waves, swimming is virtually impossible from the few beaches here.

TOP 10
2 ★★ Betancuria
3 ★★ Antigua
7 ★★ Ecomuseo de La Alcogida

Don't Miss
15 Puerto del Rosario

My Day

in the Mountain Villages away from the Coast

'Fuerte', as regular visitors call the island, is much more than simply a good seaside destination. A stroll around the former capital, a look inside Baroque village churches or a stop at a country restaurant in the shade of a date tree – the mountainous interior, away from the coastal strips, has a surprising lot to offer. A spectacular mountain road links the most attractive places with one another.

10am: Wonderful Views

The best view of the island – and one that is easy to reach – is to be had from the Mirador de Morro Velosa. Coming from Llanos de la Concepción, the viewpoint from the mountain peak at around 675m (2,200ft) can be seen from afar. From the terrace a breath-taking panoramic view opens up over ochre-coloured hilltops that have been gently eroded by the wind. In the far north you can even make out the silhouette of Fuerteventura's smaller 'sister island', Lanzarote.

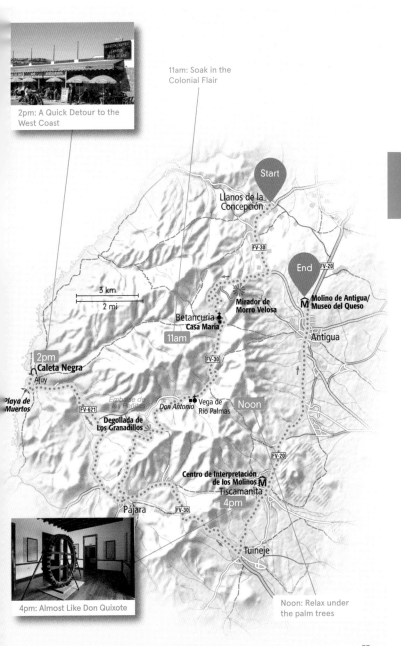

2pm: A Quick Detour to the West Coast

11am: Soak in the Colonial Flair

Start

Llanos de la Concepción

FV-30

End

FV-20

Mirador de Morro Velosa

Betancuria
Casa Maria
11am

Molino de Antigua/
Museo del Queso

Antigua

FV-30

3 km
2 mi

2pm
Caleta Negra
Ajuy

Playa de
Muertos

FV-621

Embalse de
las Peñitas

Don Antonio

Vega de
Río Palmas

Noon

Degollada de
Los Granadillos

FV-20

Centro de Interpretación
de los Molinos
Tiscamanita
4pm

Pájara

FV-30

Tuineje

4pm: Almost Like Don Quixote

Noon: Relax under the palm trees

MY DAY...

73

10am

The view from the Mirador de Morro Velosa over the surrounding hills is fantastic.

11am: Soak in the Colonial Flair

A visit to the old capital ❷ ★★ <u>Betancuria</u> in the morning is certainly a good idea as, by midday at the latest, there won't be any free parking spaces left on the road.

The Spanish conquerors chose the secluded valley as the site for their headquarters out of fear of being attacked by pirates. For almost four hundred years the fate of the island was governed from here.

Take a look inside the parish church that was built in 1410 and, between 1424 and 1431, served as the cathedral of the bishopric of Fuerteventura, as well as the grand buildings surrounding it, such as the <u>Casa María</u> which now houses the most beautiful restaurant on the island and a small ethnographic museum on the simple but harsh life led in this rural part of the island.

Noon: Relax Under the Palm Trees

Time seems to have stood still in the neighbouring village of ⓲ <u>Vega de Río Palmas</u>. A pretty pilgrimage church lies at the centre of this oasis surrounded by palm trees. The Iglesia de Nuestra Señora de la Peña was built in 1666 in the Spanish colonial style. Right next door is the country inn Don Antonio where you can take a welcome lunch break. You can either sit right on the church square

Above: Local fare and drinks are perfect at lunch time.
Right: The portal of the church of Santa María de Betancuria

with the palm leaves waving in the wind below you or in the intimate courtyard of this carefully renovated farmhouse.

Leaving the oasis and its palm trees behind you, follow the narrow mountain road that winds its way through the rugged landscape. Take a quick break at the <u>Degollada de los Granadillos</u> – at the highest point, at 434m (1,424ft) – and take in the view of the reservoir, the <u>Embalse de las Peñitas</u>, that has now almost dried up. After the top of the pass, the narrow road drops down to 21 <u>Pájara</u> and offers several other lovely viewpoints en route. There must have been lots of partridges here in the past as that is what the name of the village means in the Andalusian dialect.

This municipality at the foot of the central range of mountains is unusually well presented. This may be because it is the administrative centre for the seaside resorts on the

2pm

4pm

4pm

4pm

Top: The Playa de los Muertos in Ajuy. Above:
Camel herdsman near Tiscamanita

Jandía peninsula. The little town can even afford an outdoor swimming pool which, for a desert island, is an incredible luxury.

2pm: A Quick Detour to the West Coast

A little bit of the azure blue Atlantic is part and parcel of every excursion on Fuerteventura. **20** Ajuy on the west coast can be reached quickly from Pájara on a road that only goes to the village. It was not far from this fishing port that the Spanish Conquistadors landed around 1400.

And it wasn't long before pirates came here too on their way up the coast to Betancuria and took everything with them but the proverbial kitchen sink. A lot of blood was reputedly lost on the beach in Ajuy, the Playa de los Muertos ('Beach of the Dead').

Today, visitors come to Ajuy because of its good fish restaurants of for a walk to the white chalk cliffs and, from there, to the hidden sea caves in the Caleta Negra, the 'black bay', reached along a good path and via steep steps.

Centre, top and right: The mill museum in Antigua.
Centre bottom: Cactii and other succulents can be
admired in the botanic garden in Antigua.

4pm: Almost Like Don Quixote

From Ajuy, take the 'Windmill Route' through the centre of the island. From Tuineje you can follow the FV20 to Tiscamanita that is considered the most untouched and beautiful country village on Fuerteventura. A mill museum in a carefully restored windmill in the middle of this small village recalls the days when flour was still made with wind-power. There is a very pretty chapel in the village centre, the Ermita de San Marcos,
that dates from the 17th century. The island's cultural heritage is cherished in neighbouring ❸ ★★ <u>Antigua</u> too – one of the oldest settlements on the island. Two windmills have been beautifully restored, one of which houses a crafts museum where the craft fair 'Feria Insular de Artesanía' is held every year in May. And perhaps you will have a little bit of time on your hands to visit the cheese museum here and the little botanical garden that has been prettily laid out with prickly plants from all over the world.

❷ ★★ Betancuria

Why	Because it is the most beautiful village on the island.
Don't Miss	The historical village centre around the parish church that has been beautifully preserved.
Time	Two to three hours.
What Else	An old, roofless Franciscan monastery.
Souvenir	A piece of goat's cheese from the Finca Pepe.

View of the church Santa Maria de Betancuria

Soaking in the history and colonial flair – the former capital is the perfect place to do this. In the area around the parish church, you feel you are back in the 16th century when Betancuria was the island's capital. There are also several inviting places to have a cup of coffee or a typically Canarian lunch – but bear in mind that this is a popular tourist destination and especially busy at lunchtime.

The best way to approach Betancuria is from the south. Just as you enter the village, there's the famous picture-postcard view across the dry riverbed of the 17th-century church of Santa María, surrounded by a cluster of equally venerable bright white buildings streaked green by palm trees. The island conqueror, Jean de Béthencourt (p. 18), founded his capital here in 1404, well away from the coast, with the intention of avoiding pirate attacks. Unfortunately, the raiders were undeterred and in 1593 they destroyed the church and took 600 islanders as slaves. The village remained the capital until 1834 but thereafter became a sleepy backwater until the advent of tourism gave it a fresh lease of life.

Iglesia de Santa María

Rebuilt in 1620, this is one of the most beautiful churches on the island, with naïve-style pastel-painted side altars providing relief from the baroque high altar. The church has Gothic arches, a wineglass-shaped pulpit, a *mudéjar* ceiling, and a Judgement Day painting. Centuries-old gravestones form part of the floor, and the Norman image of St Catherine is one of the oldest post-conquest relics in the archipelago. The church is no longer used for services.

Casa Santa María

Casa Santa María is located right opposite the church. This is just a small part of the largest house in the village, much of it dating from the 16th century. It was restored by its German owner to become an island showcase in the 1990s.

An ethnographic museum where local craftspeople can be watched as they work is also part of the complex that includes the delightfully decorated restaurant with its intimate terrace and courtyard full of plants. Don't miss the multivision audio-visual show, which features the brilliant photography of Reiner Loos and Luis Soltmann.

Museo de Arte Sacro

The collection of religious art is normally housed in the colonial building opposite the Iglesia de Santa María. Since this was closed when it fell into disrepair, the most important exhibits have been displayed at the parish church.

Its highlights are the figure of Santiago (St James), brought by the Spanish in the hope that it might evangelise the Guanches, and the Pendón de la Conquista, Béthencourt's original flag.

Convento de San Buenaventura
Set 200m north of the church in a gully just off the main road is the roofless ruin of the Convento de San Buenaventura. This Franciscan abbey was the oldest on the island, founded by monks who came over with the Norman conquerors. Its roof collapsed in 1836, however, and the monks moved away.

Museo Arqueológico
This, the only archaeological collection of any importance on the island, is devoted primarily to the time before the Spanish conquest with objects from the Guanches, the indigenous inhabitants of the Canary Island. Apart from pottery, exhibits include interesting small idols made of stone. The exact purpose of these artefacts is still not known. They were discovered in the Cueva de los Idoles, a cave in a lava field near the former capital La Oliva.
The bronze cannon in the front garden was seized from the British at the Battle of Tamasite (near Tuineje). In 1740 a troop of English privateers attacked the island. The inhabitants managed to fight off the privateers and took the cannon as booty.

INSIDER TIP With a number of lovely eateries you are spoilt for choice here. The **Bodegón Don Carmelo** (p. 95) is located a little off the tourist track below the parish church. Please note that all restaurants close late in the afternoon.

 ✚ 192 C5

Iglesia de Santa María & Museo de Arte Sacro
✉ Calle Carmelo Silvera
☎ 928 878 003
🕐 Tue–Sat 10 6
💶 €2

Casa Santa María
✉ Casa Santa María Museo Artesanía
☎ 928 878 282
🕐 Mon–Sat 11–4
💶 €6

Museo Arqueológico
✉ Calle Roberto Roldán (main road)
☎ 928 862 342
🕐 Closed at present for renovation

Betancuria: Craftspeople such as weavers can be watched at work in the small museum of ethnography in the Casa Santa María.

❸ ★★ Antigua

Why	This large milling village was also the island's capital for a short time.
Don't Miss	The splendid windmill and the goat's cheese museum.
Time	One to two hours.
What Else	There is a prettily laid out botanical garden around the windmill.
Souvenir	A souvenir from Fuerteventura with a seal of authenticity.

Antigua has many things in common with its close neighbour, Betancuria, across the mountain range. It is indeed an old *(antigua)* village, established in 1485 by settlers from Normandy and Andalucía and was, for a brief period, also the island's captial. It is one of the largest farming centres. Beautifully restored, it boasts an old windmill with an adjoining cheese museum that informs visitors about the island's most important agricultural product.

Antigua boasts the most visited windmill on the island

The centre of Antigua features a charming square with the pretty white church of <u>Nuestra Señora de Antigua</u>, built in 1785.

Take a look at the <u>Casa el Portón</u> diagonally opposite. This representative gentleman's residence also dates from the 18th century. It now houses the town library. During opening hours, the pretty courtyard can be seen from a loggia.

The main attraction in Antigua is, however, the <u>Molino de Antigua</u>, a restored and fully working windmill some 200 years old, where flour was once produced to make bread and *gofio*. If you like, you can climb the very narrow stairs to see the mill's machinery more closely. It is a shame that the round granary next to the mill is not open to the public. It was originally hoped that a restaurant would open here. The <u>Museo del Queso</u>

The church of Nuestra Señora de la Antigua

Majorero in a large building adjoining informs visitors about Fuerteventura's goat's cheese that has received many awards over the years. The Fuerteventura goat *(cabra majorera)* is perfectly adapted to the barren landscape and, despite the modest supply of food, gives a surprising amount of milk. Videos explain how cheese is made and, in the next rooms, the geology of Fuerteventura is presented together with the island's native flora and fauna. Having said this, however, more could have been made out of this museum complex that was completely revamped in 2016. A wonderful view of the surrounding mountain ranges can be enjoyed from the museum's flat roof.

A small botanical garden surrounds the mill where cactii and succulents from all corners of the world can be admired alongside the flora of the Canary Islands themselves.

INSIDER TIP Apart from pizzas, the simply furnished restaurant Todo Bueno, not far from the parish church, serves mostly Canarian fare (Calle San José s/n).

✣ 193 D5

Biblioteca Municipal El Portón
✉ Calle Alcalde Montesdeoca s/n
🕐 Mon–Fri 2pm–8:30pm
(8am–2:30pm in summer)

Museo del Queso Majorero
✉ an der FV-20
☎ 928 878 041
🕐 Tue–Sat 10–5:30 🎟 €5

❼ ★★ Ecomuseo de La Alcogida

Why	Gives an idea of what Fuerteventura was like before the tourists came.
Don't Miss	A museum of ethnography where craftspeople work and live animals can be seen.
Time	Two hours.
What Else	Simple, well restored, venacular architecture.
In Short	A somewhat romantically presented view of the hard existence once eked out on this barren island.

Exhibits in the Ecomuseo de La Alcogida

This is how rural life could have looked two hundred years ago. With expert help from the University of Las Palmas de Gran Canaria, a large area in Tefía has been turned into an open-air museum aimed at making visitors acquainted with old crafts as well as the traditional way of life and rural architecture of the area. Crowing cocks, grazing sheep and mules help bring this picture to life.

The museum of ethnography is located on the road that links the two former capitals, La Oliva and Betancuria, with one another. The museum village comprises half a dozen farms and takes its name from the *alcogida*, an irrigation channel used to distribute the water drawn from wells and collected in cisterns.

Tickets should be bought at the reception before you enter the unfenced museum site. You will be given a site plan and can then explore the extensive museum area at your own pace. Each house is named after the family which lived there, in some cases until the 1970s. On the other side of the road is the Casa Señor Teodosia that reflects the former owner's affluence. The farm is made up of several different buildings and includes a mule-operated mill wheel. A threshing floor and the goats' stable lie nearby. Life in the Casa Señora Herminia was much humbler. The tiny kitchen with an open fire pit for cooking is of particular note.

Typical of all the farmhouses is the closeness between humans and animals – both living in immediate proximity to one another. Most of the outer walls are made of unhewn stone. Only at the corners could the owners afford a little luxury and added dressed stone blocks. Some of the houses are lime-washed and have simple pitched roofs. Visitors are welcome to explore inside the buildings as well where the crafts practiced by the different village residents are clearly demonstrated. In addition to a weaving room and a pottery, there is also a carpenter's workshop and an old smithy. The village did not have a central bakery. As a result, little igloo-like bread ovens can be found next to almost all the houses. Fresh bread would have been baked in these once a week. A shade-giving Peruvian peppertree was often planted next to the entrance and, between the buildings, prickly pears and spurge add a little green. A species of fig marigold grows undisturbed all over the untended fields and bathes the whole area in a rusty red when in bloom. Although this may present a romantic idyll, all in all, that rather hides the fact that life – or more precisely survival – was certainly not easy here, the museum is well-worth seeing.

INSIDER TIP The reception area includes a little café-bar. You can get a drink here and perhaps a freshly baked aniseed-flavoured bread roll. The nearest recommended restaurant is at Los Molinos (p. 89).

☩ 190 C2
✉ Tefía ☎ 928 878 049
🌐 www.majorero.com/laalcogida
🕐 Tue–Sat 10–6 💰 €5

⓯ Puerto del Rosario

Why	A visit to the island's capital is simply a must.
Don't Miss	Art in the public space everywhere.
Time	One morning when all the shops are open on the main drag.
What Else	You don't need to do without a dip in the sea when here either.
In Short	Canarian lifestyle in relatively unadulterated form.

You don't have to fall passionately in love with Puerto del Rosario. However, it would be a mistake to write off the capital simply as a mundane administrative capital. A small museum, a port where even large cruise liners call and a surprising amount of art make this town an interesting place to visit.

Puerto del Rosario has only been the island's capital since 1860. Before that time there was only a modest fishing port with a jetty and a goat's trough nearby in the large bay on the east coast. Even on maps of the island, the place was known as Puerto de Cabras ('goat's harbour'). It was only when it was recognised that things could not move forwards without a large port, that the administration was moved from Antigua to the east coast. Then a new name had to be found. In 1957 the place was finally re-christened Puerto del Rosario after the local patron saint. It still took a few years, however, before it developed into a little town.

The modern sculptures placed throughout the whole of the town centre and down the road along the shore cannot be missed. They were made from 2001 onwards as part of a sculpture symposium. Four nautilus and shell sculptures by the artist Juan Bordes occupy a prominent place on the harbour. The Centro de Arte also on the shore, named after the painter Juan Ismael,, is also well-worth a visit.

A museum opposite the parish church of Nuestra Señora del Rosario is dedicated to the Spanish poet and philosopher Miguel de Unamuno, who coined the much quoted phrase: 'Fuerteventura is an oasis in the desert of civilization'. Unamuno spent an involuntary four months in Puerto del

Rosario in 1924 after being banned to the island following his criticism of the central government in Madrid. The Palacio de Congresos, opened in 2015, forms a cultural forum for the capital.

The traffic-free Avenida Primero de Mayo, south of the church, invites visitors to stroll around and have a look. The cafés and bars here are popular meeting-places for the locals, especially in the mornings. You can unwind on the Playa de los Pozos. If, however, you have set your mind on a really good beach, the Playa Blanca just 4 km (2½mi) to the south can be recommended.

INSIDER TIP The ice cream parlour **Kiss**, on the main shopping street in the capital, not only has 20 delicious flavours to choose from but also serves an excellent white coffee (Calle Primero de Mayo 21).

Shell and nautilus sculptures add to the appeal of the harbour area.

✛ 191 E1

Oficina de Turismo
✉ Avenida Marítima s/n ☎ 618 527 668
🌐 www.turismo-puertodelrosario.org

Casa Museo Unamumo
✉ Calle Nuestra Señora del Rosario s/n

☎ 928 862 376
🕐 Mon–Fri 9–2 ✦ Free

Centro de Arte Juan Ismael
✉ Calle Almirante Lallermand 30
☎ 922 859 750
🕐 Tue–Sat 10–1, 5–9
✦ Free

The Living Desert

You need a bit of luck, admittedly. But if you time your visit perfectly, namely a few weeks after the heavy winter rains, the barren and parched plains in the island's interior are turned into a huge flowering garden with spurge, fig marigolds and garland chrysanthemums as far as the eye can see.

At Your Leisure

16 Los Molinos

A picturesque spot, popular with locals and tourists, the little fishing village of Los Molinos is one of the few places on the island where you will see fresh running water. The reason for this is a spring-fed watercourse in the Barranco de los Molinos that winds its way through the bone-dry surrounding area like a green ribbon. A footbridge crosses a shallow slow-flowing stream making its way to a small lagoon, and a flock of ducks, joined by the occasional wading bird, sits in front of the Restaurant Casa Pon. In summer the beach is golden sand; in winter the waves wash it away to uncover black shingle.

✛ 190 B2

17 Caleta de Fuste

The methodically laid out tourist town, with its big hotels, bungalow complexes and shopping centres, is built around a shallow protected bay and a busy little port. It was previously known simply as El Castillo after the Castillo de Fuste, a squat black stone watchtower built in 1741, now appropriated by the Hotel Barceló as the centrepiece of an outdoor swimming pool complex. Close by, a lighthouse made of

Ready for the tourists – on the way to Caleta de Fuste

The salt museum in Las Salinas del Carmen relates the history of salt production on Fuerteventura and provides in-depth information on sea salt and saltworks in general.

almost black volcanic stone towers above the yacht marina while, at its base, a number of smart restaurants wait for diners to arrive.

The beach is man-made but very family friendly and ideal for learning windsurfing.

✝ 193 F4

18 Salinas del Carmen

The salt pans to the south of the holiday resort Caleta de Fuste date from the 18th century when the seasalt harvested in them was the most important preservative to ensure that fish remained edible. Several of the evaporation basins, laid out like a chess board, are still used today even if only as a decorative backdrop for the Museo de la Sal where the 'white gold' can also be bought.

The saltworks, renovated with funds from the EU, is now a protected industrial monument. Outside the museum explanatory boards tell how the salt was dried, cleaned and stored in the newly restored *almacen* (warehouse), then moved on wagons on rails into boats and largely exported to the larger neighbouring islands. The former fish factory in Puerto del Rosario was the major customer from Fuerteventura in its day. The pans and the bay attract several species of wading birds and others, such as sandpipers, grey shrikes and, of course, gulls, which all benefit from the little brine shrimps that live in the salt pans.

✝ 193 F4

Museo de la Sal
☎ 928 174 926 ● Tue–Sun 10–6

19 Vega de Río Palmas

This fertile valley lives up to its name. Regardless of whether you approach it from the south or the north you will always be greeted by majestic Canarian date palms. However, the effect of the extreme lack of water can be seen on a walk through the palm groves themselves. Some of the trees have died and the reservoir, the Embalse de la Peñitas, has almost dried up after consecutive years with little rain. The jewel of this straggly scattered settlement is the village church – the Iglesia Nuestra Señora de la Peña, where a look inside is also well worthwhile. On the third Saturday in September this is the focal point for one of the island's most colourful fiestas (p. 26).

A little bit below the church square is a small road leading off to the right. Shortly after the popular restaurant for day-trippers, the Casa de la Naturaleza, a hiking trail leads to the pilgrims' chapel Ermita Virgen de la Peña (a good hour there and back). The tiny chapel is romantically located in a narrow cleft in the rocks below the dam.

✝ 192 C4

Ermita de la Virgen de la Peña
✉ Located in the centre of the village
● Tue–Sun 11–1, 5–7

20 Ajuy

In 1402 the Norman invaders, led by Jean de Béthencourt, first landed on

A steep flight of steps leads down to the Caleta Negra, the black bay near Ajuy where there are several caves, one of which can be visited.

Fuerteventura. Today it is a quiet fishing village also known by the name of Puerto Peña, mostly visited for its black sand beach, popular with surfers, and its fish restaurants. The local fishing fleet only operates between May and October, as in winter the sea is too rough.

Take a walk up the steps and along the cliff edge to see how the wind and waves have carved strange patterns. Further north you will find what is referred to as the natural monument of Caleta Negra with an impressive cave just above the water. Even experienced cave-goers should be careful when descending from here, and even more so if the sea is rough.

the interior. It is one of the island's oldest villages, settled in the 17th century and famous for its church, Nuestra Señora de la Regla, built in 1685. The carvings on the portal depict what appear to be two native Indians in headdresses, plus stylised birds and animals. These are often referred to as Aztec-influenced and

With its tiered houses, Las Playitas is one of the prettiest places in this area

while the material and the style of carving indicate a local craftsperson, the origins of the style is a mystery.

✝ 192 B4

✝ 192 C4

21 Pájara
You'll find Pájara looking spick and span and a welcome burst of floral colour after the stark brown hues of

22 Centro de Interpretación de los Molinos
This area was once the 'breadbasket' of the interior so it's an appropriate

place for a Windmill Interpretation Centre. The exhibition is in the former miller's house next to a prettily restored windmill. Apart from a variety of different hand-operated mills, exhibits include a mill originally driven by a camel (*tahona*). However, the real attraction is the windmill itself that is open to

visitors and where flour is occasionally produced. Packets of *gofio* flour are sold at the reception desk.

♁ 193 D4 ✉ Calle la Cruz 13, Tiscamanita (Tuineje) ☎ 928 164 275 🕐 Tue–Sat 10–6 💶 €2

23 Gran Tarajal/Las Playitas

After Puerto del Rosario and Corralejo, Gran Tarajal is Fuerteventura's third-largest town with a population of some 7,300. It lies in a wide, curved bay and boasts a well cared for black sandy beach and a seaside promenade lined with restaurants. As there is nowhere to stay except for one small guesthouse, this little town is only visited by a few tourists. In the evenings in particular, the locals have the place to themselves. Alternatively, you can make a beeline 6km (3.5mi) north to the little white fishing village of Las Playitas. This quaint spot nestled into the slope has a handful of popular fish restaurants. The large sports hotel nearby mostly attracts cyclists, golf players and watersports fans. From Las Playitas, a narrow no-through-road leads to the Faro de Entallada. The lookout point next to the lighthouse provides a wonderful view of the island's east coast.

♁ 164 C1/165 D2

Where to... Stay

Expect to pay per double room, per night
€   under €60
€€   €60–€90
€€€   €91–€120
€€€€ over €120

Note that many of the larger hotels and apartments in Caleta de Fuste are block booked by big tour operators.

ANTIGUA

The rooms in the Hotel Rural Era de La Corte are furnished with antiques.

Era de la Corte €€–€€€
This beautiful *hotel rural* dates from 1890 and has been lovingly restored. All 11 rooms are individually furnished and have their own style and personality – many also have direct access to the historical patio and several have four-poster beds. There is a small library, specialising in Canary Island history, flora and fauna, where guests can relax with a book and a glass of wine. Due to its remote location, a rental car is an absolute necessity.
🖙 193 D5
✉ Calle La Corte 1
☎ 928 878 705, 689 977 496
⊕ www.eradelacorte.com

CALETA DE FUSTE

Hotel Elba Palace Golf €€€€
The 5-star hotel, located in the Fuerteventura Golf Club (p. 97), features every mod con but is designed in classic Canarian style. Its large inner courtyard is decked with palms and wooden balconies and even the staff uniform is based on traditional 18th-century Canarian dress. Its 50 bedrooms are luxurious, designed with local touches, and guest facilities include two large swimming pools, a floodlit tennis (or paddle tennis) court, Jacuzzi, sauna, steam bath and beauty treatments plus a gourmet restaurant.
🖙 193 F4
✉ Urb, Fuerteventura Golf Club
☎ 928 163 922
⊕ www.hoteleselba.com

Barceló Castillo Beach Resort €€€–€€€€
Get the best of both worlds by staying in pretty little white apartments in lush manicured gardens right on the sea front, with the back-up of a huge resort-hotel. This comes complete with an entertainment programme, restaurants, and a pretty swimming pool by the 18th-century Castillo. The wonderful Thalasso Spa Centre, under the same management, lies close by the resort.
🖙 193 F4
✉ Avenida del Castillo
☎ 928 163 042 ⊕ www.barcelo.com

Fuerteventura Thalasso Spa:
☎ 928 160 961 ⏰ Daily 10–6

PÁJARA

Hotel Rural Casa Isaítas €€
This charming, friendly, small hotel, set just outside the village, has four rooms simply furnished in a 'minimalist-rustic' style. Facilities include a library, internet access and a lounge area. Its restaurant is open to non-residents and can be highly recommended.
🖙 192 C4
✉ Calle Guize 7 ☎ 928 161 402
⊕ www.casaisaitas.com

Where to... Eat and Drink

Expect to pay for a meal for one,
excluding drinks
€   under €15
€€ €15–€25
€€€ over €25

BETANCURIA

Casa Princess Arminda €€
Set in the historic heart of the village, the Casa Princess Arminda features typical Canarian dishes which are mostly home made, featuring local and sometimes home-grown ingredients. One of the restaurant's specialities is goat ragout.
✛ 165 C5
✉ Calle Juan de Bethencourt, 2
☎ 928 878 979 ⊕ www.princessarminda.com

Bodegón Don Carmelo €€
In good weather you can sit outside the door or on the patio. The platter of mixed tapas washed down with a glass of wine is always a good choice.
✛ 192 C5
✉ Calle Alcalde Carmelo Silvera 4,
☎ 928 878 391 ⦿ Sat–Thu 10–6

Casa Santa María €€€
The Casa Santa María is opposite the parish church. Great importance has been placed on creating the right atmosphere with considerable attention to detail. The small dining rooms are furnished with antiques and the courtyards with lots of plants, giving the restaurant a very personal note. House specials are rabbit and oven-baked kid.
✛ 192 C5 ✉ Plaza Iglesia
☎ 928 878 282 ⦿ Daily 11–4

Val Tarajal €€
This rustic snack bar on the through road serves tapas and standard Canarian fare ranging from meatballs (albóndigas) to rabbit. For those not so hungry, try the wrinkly potatoes with mojo sauce or a bowl of chickpea stew.
✛ 192 C5
✉ Calle Roberto Roldán 6 ☎ 928 878 007
⦿ Sun–Fri 10–4:30

PUERTO DEL ROSARIO

El Cangrejo Colorado €€
This restaurant is located in a hidden alley north of the harbour and largely serves fish and seafood. The style of the restaurant may seem a little old-fashioned but the terrace is directly on the waterfront and provides a clear view of the activities in the harbour.
✛ 191 E1
✉ Calle Juan Ramón Jimenez 2
☎ 928 858 477
⦿ Tue–Sun 1–4:30, 8–midnight

CALETA DE FUSTE

Volcano €€–€€€
A feast for the eyes as well. Whether steak, fish or a dessert, everything is imaginatively presented in this stylishly decorated restaurant. The food is not Canarian but Spanish and the wines also come primarily from the Spanish mainland.
✛ 193 F4 ✉ Centro Comercial El Castillo
☎ 928 547 645 ⊕ www.volcanorestaurant.es
⦿ Tue–Sun 1–4, 6–11:30

Chiringuito La Isla €–€€
This beach bar is on a man-made island off the Playa de la Guirra and is reached via a bridge from the mainland. Surrounded by the gentle sound of the waves, you can sit back and enjoy paella or sea bass while watching the comings and goings on the beach.
✛ 193 F4
✉ Playa de la Guirra (at the Sheraton Hotel)
☎ 928 547 893 ⦿ Daily 11–11

Caffènero €
This Italian eatery may not have a view of the sea but it serves good coffee, crêpes and pancakes as well as bruschetta and pizzas.
✛ 193 F4 ✉ Centro Comercial El Castillo
☎ 928 163 760

SALINAS DEL CARMEN

Los Caracolitos €€
This little restaurant sits almost right on the beach of this tiny fishing hamlet. There is a reasonable choice of fish and seafood dishes on the menu but if you want to go local start

The entrance to the highly regarded restaurant in the Casa Santa Maria

with the home-made fish croquettes then ask for the catch of the day.
✠ 193 F4 ✉ Salinas del Carmen
☎ 928 174 242 ● Mon–Sat noon–11

VEGA DE RÍO PALMAS

Don Antonio €€–€€€
This country inn opposite the church is a surprise. The short but choice menu offers a surprising mixture of Canarian, Spanish and international dishes.
✠ 192 C4 ✉ Plaza Iglesia ☎ 928 878 757
🌐 www.restaurantedonantonio.net
● Wed–Mom 11–5

AJUY

Jaula de Oro €
This simple beach restaurant which calls itself 'Golden Cage' is the closest to the waterfront. In a relaxed atmosphere, guests are served delicious fish dishes,.
✠ 192 B4 ☎ 928 161 594 ● Tue–Sun 10–6

PÁJARA

Bar Restaurant La Fonda €€
La Fonda is patronised by locals who drink in its rustic bar and tourists who eat outside beneath the trees. There's a selection of tapas and Canarian favourites to choose from.
✠ 192 C4 ✉ Calle Nuestra Señora de Regla
☎ 928 161 625 ● Mon–Fri 9–6, Sat, Sun 9–9

Centro Cultural €
In this restaurant you will enjoy local cuisine, which includes the usual favourites such as kid and rabbit, accompanied by an island wine from Tenerife or Lanzarote.
✠ 192 C4 ✉ Plaza del Ayuntamiento
☎ 928 161 440 ● Daily 8am–midnight

LAS PLAYITAS

Casa Victor €€
This is by no means the most attractive restaurant in Las Playitas but even when the rest of the village is deserted Victor's is buzzing. The fish cooked on a hot stone and traditionally served with wrinkly potatoes is good.
✠ 193 D2 ✉ Calle Juan Soler 22
☎ 928 870 910 ● Tue–Sun noon–5, 8–11

Where to... Shop

BETANCURIA

Canarian handicrafts as well as simple trinkets can be found in the souvenir shop near the church that belongs to the Casa Santa Maria. It also stocks a good range of ceramic products, printed t-shirts and jams, mojo and other culinary specialities from the island.

On the southern edge of the village is the Casa de Queso, selling a range of cheeses.

Just outside the villages in the local cheese maker Finca Pepe (Granja la Acaravaneras, daily 10–6; www.fincapepe.com), where you can sample and buy the local goat's cheese.

ANTIGUA

Handcrafted items made on Fuerteventura are sold in the Artesanía de Fuerteventura in the Museo del Queso Majorero. Of particular note are the woven baskets, bags made of palm leaves, traditional hats, olive oil made in the neighbouring village Tiscamanita and goat's cheese.

PUERTO DEL ROSARIO

Take a stroll along Calle Primero de Mayo and Calle León y Castillo, though most of the shops are old-fashioned and uninspiring. One exception is Las Rotondas (Calle Francisco Pi y Arsuaga 2), which is the largest consumer temple on the island.

On the second Sunday of March, June, September and December (10:30–2:30) a craft market is held in the village of Tetir 8km (5mi) west of Puerto del Rosario.

CALETA DE FUSTE

Despite, or perhaps because of its many shopping centres, the standard of shopping in Caleta de Fuste is mediocre and usually price driven. The best shopping centre is the Atlántico directly on the main road.

Souvenirs and handicrafts are sold at a mercadillo with some 200 different stalls held on Tuesdays and Saturdays from 10 am until 2pm.

Riu Parfum in the Centro Comercial El Castillo is the best bet for perfumes and aloe vera products.

Where to... Go Out

NIGHTLIFE

Good places to go in the evening are Caleta de Fuste, the Blues Bar in Centro Castillo and Luna Blue, a cocktail lounge with live music

on the main road (Avenida Juan Ramón Soto Morales).

Of course for the real action, you need to go to the island capital of Puerto del Rosario. Young city dwellers go to the Mama Rumba (Calle San Roque 7).

There are 90 different beers to choose from at the Heineken Bar (Calle León y Castillo 146). La Tierra (Calle Eustaqio Gopar) has live jazz on Friday and Saturday.

GOLF

For golf players, Caleta de Fuste, an 18-hole course, is the top address on the island.

Professional players also use the Fuerteventura Golf Club (tel: 928 160 034; www.fuerteventuragolfclub.com) in the south of the holiday resort.

Not far away is the Salinas de Antigua (tel: 928 877 272; www.salinasgolf.com), another 18-hole golf course, which also has a golf hotel and golf school.

And then there is also the Las Playitas Golf (18-holes; tel: 928 860 401; www.playitas.net) course near Gran Tarajal.

SEA EXCURSIONS

The catamaran sailing boat run by Obycat Experience (www.obycat.com) departs every day from the yacht marina in Caleta de Fuste. It normally sails to the bay of Pozo Negro where you can snorkel or swim.

WATER SPORTS

The bay of Caleta de Fuste is an ideal place to take your first windsurfing lessons. Surfing and stand-up paddling courses for beginners are offered at the Canary Surf Academy (www.canarysurfacademy.com).

For diving contact Deep Blue (tel: 928 163 712; www.deep-blue-diving.com) next to the yacht marina.

HORSERIDING

The Finca Crines del Viento (tel: 609 001 141; www.crinesdelviento.es) stables at Triquivijate offers rides suitable for beginners and experienced riders.

The south coast on the Jandía peninsula
is famous for the most beautiful, golden,
sandy beaches in the Canary Islands.

The South

Wind and waves, virtually endless beaches – the south of Fuerteventura is arguably the best seaside destination in the Canary Island.

Pages 98–127

Getting Your Bearings

Even the once difficult access is a thing of the past. A fast road now links the seaside resorts in the south of the island with the airport some 80km (50mi) away in little more than an hour. On Fuerteventura, the south means – first and foremost – Jandía. Long, golden sandy beaches, extending in all to around 30km (18mi), attract beach-lovers and watersports enthusiasts to this large peninsula all year round. Despite the many new hotels and holiday clubs that have opened in the past few years there is still room for everyone down on the beach.

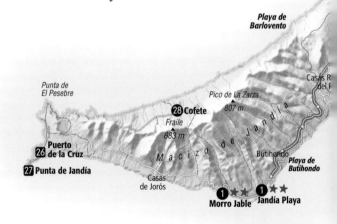

The new face of the south is Costa Calma, a man-made resort bristling with large modern hotels and shopping centres. On the beaches on the Jandía isthmus to the south west, tourism is focused around Jandía

Playa. This seaside town has mushroomed into a large holiday resort over the last 40 years and merged with neighbouring Morro Jable. The advantage of this holiday region is that unlike the north of

Fuerteventura, which can become quite cloudy, the sun shines on the isthmus for almost 365 days a year, which makes it ideal for beach and surfing holidays. Windsurfers and kiteboarders rave about the good wind conditions on the Playa Barca.

The north coast (Barlovento) of the isthmus provides a contrast to the holiday centres on the Playas de Jandía. You will hardly see a soul in this region, no hotel buildings have yet disfigured the mile-long beaches of Cofete.

The palm grove of La Lajita is like an oasis in this arid semi-desert landscape, beyond which is the Oasis Park with its colourful ornamental plants and animals. This zoo is the largest on the Canary Island and you can easily spend a whole day here.

My Day
on a 4 × 4 Public Bus Service to the End of the Island

Do you want to get away from your hotel beach, just once, and visit a really untouched dream beach? You do? Since just recently, you don't even need a hire car to do this. The Playa de Cofete on the remote north side of the Jandía peninsula can be reached on a public bus, or more precisely in a 4×4 vehicle that can cope with the bumps and potholes without a problem.

🕙 **10am: Ride off into the Desert!** The tour starts at the bus station in ❶ ★★ <u>Morro Jable</u> – but get there early. The 21 seats in the Unimog bus are generally taken pretty quickly. Shortly after passing the harbour the road turns into a bumpy track like driving over corrugated sheet metal. The treeless landscape seems to be even drier here than elsewhere on the island. Protected by the Jandía range it virtually never rains here.

🕚 **11am: The Last Bar on the Edge of Civilisation** Coming over the pass a spectacular panorama unfolds in front of you

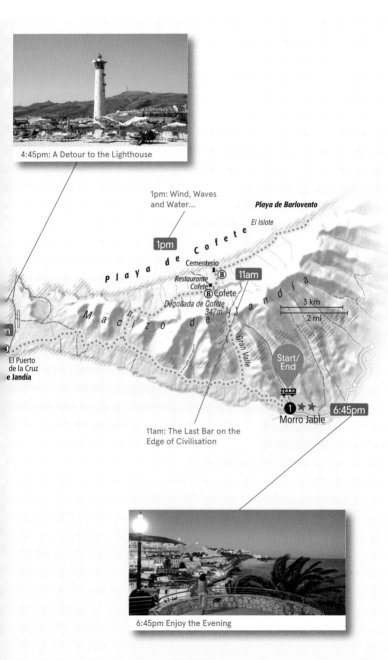

4:45pm: A Detour to the Lighthouse

1pm: Wind, Waves and Water...

Playa de Barlovento

El Islote

1pm

P l a y a   d e   C o f e t e

Cementerio Ⓑ

Restaurante Cofete ■
Ⓑ Cofete 11am

Degollada de Cofete
347m

M a c i z o   d e   *J a n d í a*

3 km
2 mi

Gran Valle

Start/
End

El Puerto
de la Cruz
e Jandía

Morro Jable ★★ 6:45pm

11am: The Last Bar on the
Edge of Civilisation

6:45pm Enjoy the Evening

Goats are everywhere (above). The Playa del Matorral with Morro Jable lighthouse (left).

of the Playa de Cofete. The place **28** Cofete itself is a collection of the most basic of huts that were in fact inhabited up until the 1960s and finally abandoned. Since then, the 'Cofete' has enjoyed a monopoly here – and, rather cockily, even calls itself a restaurant. If there is anything such as authentic Canarian cooking, then here. Tablecloths, menus – no chance! And paying with a card is an absolute no go. Whatever is available on any day

is written on a slate board – generally a paella or the much more substantial goat ragout in a spicy sauce. And fish, of course!

1pm: Wind, Waves and Water…
From the bar it is a 15-minute hike to the Playa de Cofete. You can watch the endless surge of the waves on this completely undeveloped beach of superlatives. The waves roll in slowly and seemingly harmlessly on this wide sandy beach – but don't

If you don't come here on the Unimog bus, you can drive right down to the beach on an off-road jeep.

let yourself be deceived. Swimming here is almost always dangerous and there have repeatedly been accidents and people have lost their lives here. It's best just to cool your feet on the very edge of the water. The fine sandy *playa* is just perfect, however, for beach walks, barefoot of course. Once you have passed the old cemetery of Cofete that is, rather strangely, almost right on the shore, then you will find yourself really on your own. And what a backdrop!

The Jandía mountains tower up to a height of 800m (2,625ft) with their steep and rugged flanks dropping down into the sea below.

2pm: Simply Wonderful!
After an hour you will reach El Islote, a flat rocky isle in the sea facing the beach. As you get nearer you will notice that it is connected to the mainland by a sandbank. Make the effort and clamber up onto the island – but be quiet. Most of the

Top: A cross on a grave in the old cemetery in Cofete Above: The Jandía mountains tower up above the beach.

time you will not be alone here – rock crabs the size of your hand splash around in the wash of the waves.

The beach beyond El Islote is called the Playa de Barlovento.

As long as you still have time or intend to return to Morro Jable on foot anyway, you shouldn't miss a longer hike along the beach where you will find yourself really far from anywhere.

The island's tallest lighthouse is in Morro Jable.

🕐 **4:45pm: A Detour to the Lighthouse**

When on the Playa de Cofete you don't need to go all the way back to the bus stop in Cofete itself but can get on at the cemetery. The return journey includes a little surprise as the bus does not take the direct route back to Morro Jable but makes a slight detour to the hamlet **26** Puerto de la Cruz and, from there, to the lighthouse Faro de Jandía in the most southwesterly corner of the island.

🕐 **6:45pm Enjoy the Evening**

Round off the day in one of the cosy restaurants in Morro Jable.

❶ ★★ Jandía Playa & Morro Jable

Why	Fuerteventura's best and most popular seaside resort.
Don't Miss	The endless beach.
Time	One whole day.
What Else	Excellent fish restaurants can be found on the promenade in Morro Jable.
In Short	Knowing that you can have a wonderful day on the beach virtually every day of the year.

The Playas de Jandía are picture-postcard perfect

What an amazing sandy paradise! The beaches known by the collective name Playas de Sotavento stretch for 30km (18mi) from Costa Calma to Morro Jable on the south coast of Jandía peninsula. For most holiday-makers they are the very reason for coming to Fuerteventura, regardless of whether you want to relax on the beach or do watersports. And just a stone's throw from life on the beach is the surprising, fragile beauty of a mountainous region untouched by human hand.

Jandía Playa

The principle resort on the peninsula visited largely by German holiday-makers is Jandía Playa. The holiday centre merged long ago with the neighbouring village Morro Jable that itself evolved around a small fishing village. Basically speaking, Jandía Playa comprises one long boulevard, the Avenida del Saladar, with lots of shopping malls and countless hotel complexes that have spread inland away from the road. Those in the second and third rows are on the slopes of the Jandía mountains themselves. The Playa del Matorral is the hub of holiday life and is wide enough to provide space for everyone under one of the sunshades laid out in perfect rows, even in high season in summer and at Christmas time. The 59m (194ft)-tall lighthouse halfway along the beach has become the town's most famous landmark. Miraculously,

the salt marsh (el saladar) between the boulevard and the beach – now a designated conservation area – has been spared from development. The fenced in area floods regularly and provides an ecological habitat for salt-loving plants. Visitors are requested not to leave the plank footpath on their way to the sea. To the west, on the Playa del Matorral, the Robinson Club Jandía Playa opened in 1970 as the very first holiday club. Thanks to its exceptional location it has been popular ever since and can rely on a faithful number of regular guests

View of the wide Playa del Matorral in the early evening.

Holiday clubs
and hotel
complexes
line the
Jandía Playa.

from Germany. In the east, below the Aldiana club village on the cliffs, the Playa del Matorral seamlessly runs into the Playa de Butihondo. So far, no special sunbeds zone have been created here on this narrow and partly pebbly stretch of sand that extends for some 1.5 km (1 mi). It is mostly frequented by walkers who carry on as far as the much visited Playa de Esquinzo. Other large holiday clubs and hotel complexes can be found at the top of the cliffs. Flights of steps connect these to the beach that is divided into two by the Barranco de Esquinzo.

Morro Jable

A wonderful seaside promenade starts to the west of the Robinson Club and leads to Morro Jable, running along below the hotels on the cliffs. One fish restaurant next to another can be found here. Just past the restaurant La Laja a flight of steps takes you to Nuestra Señora del Carmen, the parish church of Morro Jable. The church itself is unusually plain but from the square outside there are lovely views over the holiday resort and the beach.

The small Old Town of Morro Jable with its narrow alleyways was virtually the only noteworthy settlement on the Jandía peninsula, together with the hamlet of Cofete, until the tourists arrived. The local beach serving Morro, as most people call it now, is the Playa de Cebada below the seaside promenade – its golden yellow sand marks the western end of the some 30 km (18½ mi)-long beach of superlatives around Jandía.

Ferries to Gran Canaria depart from the harbour to the west of the town centre every day. You can also book catamaran trips from here and travel up and down the coast. In a breeding and rescue station for turtles on the harbour wall (Centro de recuperatión y conservación de tortugas marinas),

turtles injured by the propellers of boats are nursed back to health. The station, however, has not been spruced up for visitors. Several of these impressive and unusual marine animals can usually be seen in one of the large basins.

The Jandía mountain ridge dominates the south of the peninsula of the same name.

Jandía Nature Reserve

The Parque Natural de Jandía, largely made up of the mountain ridge, provides a backdrop for the magnificent beach scenery on both sides of the Jandía peninsula. The nature reserve stretches from the isthmus Istmo de La Pared near

Costa Calma to the lighthouse at the Punta de Jandía in the most southwesterly corner of the peninsula. The often jagged mountain ridge drops relatively steeply on both sides. From Jandía Playa, the highest point – the Pico de la Zarza at 812m (2,664ft) – can be reached comfortably in around 2½ hours. The good hiking trail starts a few hundred yards above Hotel

Succulents are a characteristic feature in this dry climate.

Barceló Jandía Playa. Enjoy the spectacular panorama views of the completely undeveloped beach at Cofete and the north side of the peninsula from the top of the mountain. A number of endemic plants can be seen at the top of the Pico de la Zarza in early spring, including the mountain goldstar. Take lots of drinking water with you and something to eat on this hike – the difference in altitude is a good 800 m (2625ft) – and there are no facilities en route.

INSIDER TIP There are several good beach bars on the Playas de Sotavento which serve snacks and cold drinks. The terrace of the **Beach Bar El Faro** on the Playa de Matorral next to the lighthouse is a relaxing place to sit with your back to the holiday resort Jandía.

 ✠ 194 C1

Centro de recuperación y conservación de tortugas marinas
🕐 Mon–Fri 10–1 🎟 Free

❽ ★★ La Lajita Oasis Park

Why	The only zoo on Fuerteventura is also the largest on the Canary Islands.
Don't Miss	The cheeky meerkats or the charming elephants.
Time	Half, or better, a whole day.
What Else	A farmers' market that also sells handicrafts is held near the zoo on Sundays.
In Short	A good day out with a large garden-centre adjoining.

Visitors to the Oasis Park can watch graceful gazelles, marvel at the mid-flight acrobatics of birds of prey or interact with sea lions and lemurs – just as you like. A botanical garden adjoins the largest zoo on the Canary Islands which boasts an opulent display of sub-tropical ornamental plants as well as rare species endemic to the Canaries.

The park features pink flamingos and a lush display of plants.

Visitors are surprised by the lush green of the palm grove near the entrance and the sub-tropical plants from all over the world – not what one might expect on a desert island like Fuerteventura! At the ticket desk you will be given a flyer with the times of the shows with the sea lions, the birds of prey and the parrots. All animal and bird shows are included in the entrance fee. If you book additional attractions such as a camel safari or an personal meeting with a sea lion, for example, these can cost quite a lot of money in addition to the already not inexpensive standard admission price. To make it worthwhile, make use of the whole day and arrive

A camel ride is a must for many visitors.

early. Free bus services run from all parts of the island, even from Corralejo 90km (56mi) away. Shuttle buses take visitors from one attraction to another in this huge park. Or you can hire an electro scooter and drive around the park as you please.

Experience Animals Close Up

What are the stars among the 3,000 animals in the Oasis Park? There are lots of different ones that can be picked out: size-wise these are certainly the elephants and the giraffes. But the porcupines, the cheeky meerkats and the strutting pink flamingos are not to be left out either. And if you want that very special holiday picture there are professional photographers on hand to take a shot of you with an owl or a lemur eating out of your hand. With regard to how the animals are kept and trained – of course, like every other zoo, not all the demands of animal rights campaigners can be met. Some of the enclosures seem a little small and does a parrot really need to be taught how to ride a bicycle and other tricks? Nobody doubts about the courage of the crocodile tamer when he sticks his head between the animal's jaws. And there are all sorts of positive things here, too. The bird show works with birds of prey that could not survive here in a natural environment. One of the Oasis Park's special priorities is to help save certain species of animal from extinction. The Cuvier's gazelle breeding programme has been especially successful. A number of gazelles born in the park have been released into the wild in their native Atlas Mountains. The wetlands and banks of ponds within the park have become an important habitat for breeding and migrating birds. The park is particularly proud of areas created like the African savannah where the herds of giraffes live alongside antelopes and zebras.

Botanic Discoveries

The elephants, hippos and monkeys are the main attractions of the park. However, for the botanically minded, a walk through the botanic garden is just as interesting. Depending on the season, acacias, tulip and orchid trees may be in bloom. Cactii and other succulents, which thrive in this dry climate, form a special section of their own. The upper part of the garden is reserved for local flora. In total, the botanical collection comprises around 1,500 different species of plants.

INSIDER TIP The range of food sold in the park is not the best. For good fish, for example, try the beach restaurant **Ramón** (Avenida Fragata 13, Tel. 928 87 21 26, closed Thurs.) in La Lajita.

✠ 195 E3
✉ Carretera General de Jandía
(FV2 km 57.4), La Lajita
☎ 902 400 434 ⊕ www.lajitaoasispark.com
🕐 Daily 9–6
💶 €35, children €20.50.
Separate charge for camel rides

ⓘ

㉔ Costa Calma

Why	This part of the Playas de Sotavento has arguably one of the best resorts on the island.
Don't Miss	The superb swimming and surfing or a walk along the beach
Time	Enough to have an enjoyable swim or to relax on the beach.
What Else	Sandy hiking trails leading inland.
In Short	They don't come much better than this.

In many spots the Costa Calma lives up to its name

It is no longer as quiet here as the name Costa Calma ('quiet coast') suggests. However, compared to Morro Jable further to the south or Corralejo in the north of Fuerteventura things here are certainly a little more peaceful on this stretch of the coast. The big plus points in this expansive holiday resort are the magnificent beaches and popular surfing spots just outside the door.

Coming from the north, this holiday resort is, so to speak, the gateway to the Jandía peninsula. 50 years ago, there wasn't even a fishing village on this stretch of coast – even the name Costa Calma didn't exist. For this reason don't expect to find an old village centre. The first residential units were built in the 1970s; today, the resort has more than 15,000 beds. Building activity has diminished in the meantime although there are several sites waiting to be used between the holiday flat complexes and the large hotels. Everything has been very generously laid out, albeit with little imagination. A fortunate bit of planning was the green strip alongside the through road that is simply referred to as El Palmeral ('the palm grove') and is an inviting spot for a walk in the shade. The planting of predominantly Canarian date palms and quick-growing casuarina trees was begun in 1986. Today, the grove lines the road over a length of almost 2 km (1¼ mi). They are watered in a resource-enhancing method, namely with waste water from the hotels.

Windsurfers and those who want to try their hand are in the perfect place on the Costa Calma.

A Paradise for Swimmers and Surfers

In Costa Calma people don't stroll along the streets where the shops are or along the seaside promenade but on the sandy beach Playa de Costa Calma itself that stretches 2km (1¼ mi) from Sotavento Beach Club to Playa Barca. The light-coloured sandy beach which boasts a Blue Flag certification, slopes gradually into the sea. Many sun-seekers protect themselves from the wind that picks up especially in the afternoon, behind rows of stones or mounds of sand. Windsurfers and kiteboarders, on the other hand, are in their element here, particularly on the Playa Barca where you can hire the necessary equipment at René Egli's windsurfing centre where there is also a wide range of courses for beginners. The Hotel

Meliá Fuerteventura (formerly Meliá Gorriones) that lies directly above the beach is also popular among non-surfers due to its solitary location. At low tide, a huge, shallow lagoon is formed right in front of the hotel with a mile-long sandbank dividing it from the open sea and acting as a wave-breaker. The water in the lagoon shimmers all shades of blue and turquoise and draws lines across the gold-coloured sand. At Risco del Paso, to the south of Playa Barca, the wind has formed two huge migrating dunes. The

best way to these natural wonders is on a one-hour walk along the beach from the Hotel Meliá Fuerteventura.

Crossing the Island
Costa Calma is located at the narrowest point on Fuerteventura,

The sandy beaches can equally well be explored by bike.

the Istmo de la Pared, an isthmus, as the name implies. The island here is just 5km (3mi) wide. Equipped with comfortable hiking shoes, sun cream and plenty of drinking water, you can head out from the El Palmeral shopping centre and cross the peninsula in a good hour and carry on along the rocky coastline in the west either to the north or south, as you like (p. 172).

INSIDER TIP Walkers on the Playas de Sotavento can find shady beach bars every half an hour where they can get cold drinks or a little something to eat. The **Beachbar Horizonte** (on a level with the Monica Beach Resort) is a wonderful place with chairs right on the sand.

ℹ 🕂 192 A1

At Your Leisure

25 La Pared

The site of the wall that once divided the island into two ancient kingdoms (p. 19). Originally, a large holiday complex was supposed to have been built here. However, the ambitious plans never came to anything and, as a result, day-trippers are confronted with an unfinished building site with bumpy roads and battered streetlights. The wild and romantic Playa del Viejo Rey ('Old King's Beach'), on the other hand, is magnificent. Big waves crash onto this natural beach and surfers are totally in their element here. The fish restaurant Bahía La Pared (p. 124) has an inviting terrace from where you can experience wonderful sunsets). Drive a little further north on the FV605 past the village turn-off and a superb panorama of the north coast opens out before you.

✝ 167 E3

Beach restaurant near Le Pared

Taking things slowly in Puerto de la Cruz

26 Puerto de la Cruz

El Puertito is the name given to this tiny fishing port by the locals. It is located some 22 bumpy kilometres (13½ mi) west of Morro Jable. Three rustic fish restaurants have made it a popular place to visit. From here, a narrow lane leads to a miniature lighthouse at Punta Pesebre from where you can hike along the north coast of the Jandía peninsula.

✝ 194 A1

27 Punta de Jandía

The Faro de Punta Jandía on the island's southwestern-most point helps ships on their way. Operation started in 1864, making it the oldest

The remotely situated Villa Winter

single-track hairpin bends with unprotected drops, is truly hair-raising! Slow down, use your horn on blind bends and be very careful. As you pass the highest point of the journey, shortly after the mountain pass Degollada de Agua Oveja at the Mirador de Barlovento, your reward is a view far along the north-west coast that will linger long in your memory. This is an awesome landscape unchanged in eons, on which man has made very little impression.

The ramshackle hamlet of Cofete with its café-restaurant is for many people the end of the line. Here they enjoy a well-earned cup of coffee, perhaps a meal and head back with a satisfying 'been there, seen it' feeling.

From the restaurant you can look out to the mansion of Gustav Winter, which sits isolated and brooding beneath the mountains. Low clouds often hang menacingly here and there is a real sense of drama. Little wonder that this has become the most talked about house on the island. Although it is only a short drive to the mansion do not attempt it unless you have a 4WD vehicle as the road is very bumpy indeed.

lighthouse on the Canary Islands. It is situated on a little hillock from which lovely views can be enjoyed. In good weather, the silhouette of Gran Canaria can even be seen.

✛ 194 A1

28 Cofete

The road to Cofete begins promis-ingly, just south of Morro Jable, with brand new asphalt roads. Alas, these last barely 3km (2mi) and then it is another 24km (15mi) of teeth-rattling, spine-jolting, dirt-track driving. The last part of the journey, on little more than

✛ 194 B2

Tourist office Jandía Playa
✉ Centro Comercial Cosmo
☎ 928 540 776 ◑ Mon–Fri 9–3

Sundowner in La Pared

To watch the sunset, you have to go from one side of the island to the other if you are staying in the resorts on the east coast. From the Costa Calma it is just a hop, skip and jump to La Pared on the romantically wild west coast. Drive through the settlement that looks as if it hasn't been completed, heading for the restaurant Bahía La Pared (tel: 928 549 030). Unwind on the terrace and enjoy watching the deep red sun dip down into the sea behind the cliffs. And just by the way – it's a good idea to book a table in advance.

Where to... Stay

Expect to pay per double room, per night
€   under €60
€€   €60–€90
€€€   €91–€120
€€€€   over €120

JANDÍA PLAYA

Faro Jandía €€€
Standing opposite the landmark *faro* (light-house) and set back from the main road, this 4-star hotel offers 214 spacious rooms to a mainly package-tour clientele. Nightly evening entertainment, three artificial grass tennis courts and the free use of a neigh-bouring Spa and Wellness Centre help to make this one of the resort's most popular hotels.
⊹ 194 C1 ✉ Avenida del Saladar 17
☎ 928 545 035
⊕ www.murhotels.com

Iberostar Fuerteventura Palace €€€€
This hotel, operated by the Spanish Iberostar chain, is one of the few hotels in Jandía with direct access to the beach. Another plus point, in addition to the opulent buffet, is the very well-maintained spa facility. The diving school in the hotel also offers courses for beginners. Following a complete over-haul in 2018, the former 4-star hotel gained another star and is only open to adult guests.
⊹ 194 C1 ✉ Urb. Las Gaviotas
☎ 928 540 444 ⊕ www.iberostar.com

Robinson Club Jandía Playa €€€€
Established in 1970, this was the famous German club's first ever venture and the first club-resort complex of its kind on the island. Today its pioneering spirit might seem rather out of place amid the high rises and amusement arcades. It has been developed and extended, and has always had access to one of the best stretches of the Playa Mattoral. In 2018 an 11-storey *torre* with an infinity pool on the roof was added. It offers a high standard of service and guests have a wide choice of different leisure and entertainment facilities. The resort is re-nowned for its excellent sports and water sports programmes. There are 10 tennis courts as well as courses in windsurfing, catamaran sailing and diving. There is an-other Robinson Club nearby, at Esquinzo.
⊹ 194 C1 ✉ Avenida del Saladar
☎ 928 169 100 ⊕ www.robinson.com

COSTA CALMA

Bungalows Risco del Gato €€€€
The architecture of this luxury resort that opened in the 1990s has lost nothing of its extravagance. The 51 white bungalows, which the architect intended to represent North African houses, comprise a conven-tional bedroom, a round pod-like bathroom featuring a large porthole window. Each suite has its own private patio and a hemi-spherical sitting room overlooking the gardens. There are two pools on different levels and the beautifully landscaped grounds provide a real feeling of space for its guests. The complex includes an elegant Thai spa and an à-la-carte-restaurant of gourmet standard.
⊹ 195 D3 ✉ Calle Sicasumbre 2
☎ 928 547 175 ⊕ www.vikhotels.com

Río Calma €€€€
Set high on a hill to the north, overlooking the whole resort, at first glance this build-ing resembles a large church. A glass lift in the shape of a fairy-tale castle turret takes you to the accommodation area and now you are in colonial Spain, with pastel-washed colonnaded streets and houses. Screw pines, casuarina trees and other sub-tropical plants can be admired in the pretty gardens. Most of the 416 rooms have a view of the sea. For sports-minded guests there are several tennis courts and a mini-golf course.
⊹ 195 D3 ✉ El Granillo
☎ 928 546 050 ⊕ www.r2hotels.com

ESQUINZO

Club Jandía Princess €€€€
Inspired by Moorish architecture and completely white-washed, this all-inclusive hotel is in a peaceful and very attractive location slightly above the wonderful sandy

beach, the Playa de Esquinzo, which can be reached down a short flight of steps. With more than 500 rooms, it is one of the largest hotel complexes on Fuerteventura. The rooms are divided into a family-friendly part and another reserved for adults only. It is well-worth paying a little extra for a room with a view of the sea. An extensive sports programme ensures that nobody gets bored. Aerobics and archery, for example, are included in the price. Windsurfing and sailing courses can be booked for an additional fee.

⊹ 194 C1 ✉ Urb. Esquinzo Butihondo
☎ 928 544 089, 902 406 306
⊕ www.princess-hotels.com

MORRO JABLE

Hotel XQ El Palacete €€€
With just 54 rooms, of which two are junior suites, the El Palacete is one of the smaller hotel complexes on Fuerteventura. The two-floor complex overlooks the beach of Morro Jable – just across the pedestrian promenade and down some steps. There is a wonderful view of the sea and the resort from all the rooms. No loud entertainment programmes disturb guests looking for peace and quiet.

⊹ 194 C1 ✉ Acantilado s/n
☎ 928 542 070
⊕ www.xqelpalacete.com

PLAYA BARCA

Club Aldiana €€€€
Renowned for its sports, spa and wellness facilities, the German-run Club Aldiana is one of the pioneers on Jandía peninsula, arriving here in the late 1970s. It is set in attractive grounds that tumble down to a beautiful stretch of beach where there is a diving school, and a fish restaurant. Most of its bungalows are fairly simple though there is a handful of newer luxury units too.

⊹ 195 D2 ✉ Playa de Jandía
☎ 928 169 870 ⊕ www.aldiana.de

Meliá Fuerteventura €€€–€€€€
From an architectural point of view, there are doubtless nicer looking hotels on Fuerteventura, but the hotel's location on Playa Barca, one of the island's most famous beaches, is absolutely phenomenal. Not surprisingly, the rooms at the Meliá are always in demand. Surfers love the place. Its facilities are excellent, and the extensive mature grounds include four pools, one tennis court, a health centre and a gym. The famous Pro Centre René Egli Windsurf School is also based here. The first row of Casas del Mar apartments in the recently extended building complex offer great comfort and wonderful views.

⊹ 195 D2 ✉ Playa Barca
☎ 928 547 025 ⊕ www.melia.com

The pools at the Hotel XQ El Palacete

Where to... Eat and Drink

Expect to pay for a meal for one,
excluding drinks

€   under €15
€€   €15–€25
€€€   over €25

LA LAJITA

Ramón €–€€
A simple eatery in a nice location right next
to the church on the sea road, opposite the
pebbly beach. While tourists generally sit on
the outdoor terrace, the bar inside is taken
over by the locals who drop in for a *cortado*
or an beer.
✝ 195 E3
✉ Avenida Fragata 13
☎ 928 872 126 ● Fri–Wed 11–11

LA PARED

Bahía La Pared €€
This beachside fish restaurant enjoys
tremendous views and is very popular with
locals and families, not least because there's
a play area for children including a small
pool with waterslides. The food is also
excellent. If you're not sure which fish to
choose ask the waiter for a recommenda-
tion. Book a table on the terrace, get here
early evening and watch the sunset.
✝ 195 D4
✉ Playas de la Pared
☎ 928 549 030 ● Daily noon–10

COSTA CALMA

B-Side €€
The Italian restaurant on the top floor of the
Bahía Calma Shopping Center is one of the
most popular places in the area. Although a
little bit back from the beach you can enjoy
a view over the sea from the tables at the
windows while enjoying your spaghetti or
crisp, brick-oven baked pizza. The service,
however, leaves much to be desired.
✝ 195 D3
✉ Calle Punta del Viento s/n
☎ 928 549 140
● Mon–Sat 1–11:30

Mediterran €€
This restaurant in the centre of the Las Abejas
apartment complex (besides the Centro
Comercial El Palmeral) is not the easiest
place to find. As the name clearly indicates,
the cuisine has a Mediterranean focus.
Specialities include not only steaks and
pasta but also lamb dishes, while gazpacho
and minestrone are typical starters. Very
relaxing atmosphere.
✝ 195 D3
✉ Calle Playa de la Jaqueta s/n
☎ 699 136 840 ● Daily from 5pm

Posada San Borondon I €€
This rustic bodega with its wine barrel décor
could be anywhere on the Spanish mainland.
And just as in Spain, platters of manchego
cheese and serrano ham are also served
here, too. Almost every day the landlord
himsef plays live music to add to the atmosphere. Just sit back and enjoy yourself with
a carafe of sangria.
✝ 195 D3
✉ Centro Comercial Sotavento
☎ 928 547 100
● Daily 11am–1:30am

La Terraza del Gato €€
In this restaurant near the Hotel Risco del
Gato you can expect good, hearty Canarian
cooking. As a starter, you can choose between classics such as melon and serrano
ham, fried Padrón peppers *(pimientos de
padrón)* or shrimps in garlic sauce; juicy
Argentinian beef steaks are prepared on the
grill and fish dishes are served with wrinkly
potatoes.
✝ 195 D3
✉ Calle Sicasumbre ☎ 677 414 279
⊕ www.terrazadelgato.eu
● Daily noon–10

ESQUINZO

Marabú €€
The family-run Marabú ('Feathers'), is tucked
away between the main road and the beach
of Esquinzo in a charming garden terrace
courtyard in a modern development. The
interior boasts many traditional elements yet
is also light, modern and inviting. The chef

Paella – that tasty Valencian rice dish served in a pan – is also on the menu of the Restaurant Saavedra Clavijo

Ralf Johmann favours the international cuisine. The extensive wine menu lists several from the Spanish mainland but also some from neighbouring Lanzarote. Advance booking is recommended especially in the evening.

✠ 194 C1
✉ Calle Fuente de Hija
☎ 928 544 098 ⊕ www.e-marabu.com
🕐 Mon–Sat 1–11

JANDÍA PLAYA

China Town €–€€
If you don't fancy anything Spanish or Canarian and stil want a cheap meal, then head for China Town. It is one of the few Asian restaurants in the south. The extensive menu includes twelve duck dishes alone. If you are a larger group then you mix and match a meal of several courses. The eatery is in a side street off the Avenida del Saladar (level with the Ifa Hotel Altamarena).

✠ 194 C1
✉ Calle Bentejuy 9 (Edificio Esmeralda)
☎ 928 541 601
🕐 Daily 11:30–11:30

MORRO JABLE

Saavedra Clavijo €€
As so often, it is the location of a restaurant that counts – and this fish restaurant right on the seaside promenade cannot complain that it doesn't get enough guests! Specialities include fish soup and paella with shellfish for two; the fresh fish (pescada fresca Morro Jable) is always good. Meat dishes here are not the main attraction.

✠ 194 C1 ✉ Avenida Tomás Grau Gurrea 6
☎ 928 166 080 🕐 Daily 10am–midnight

La Farola del Mar €€
This restaurant is squeezed in at the west end of the string of eateries in Morro Jable and, like all the others, has a few tables right on the water, too. The big difference here is that it is quiet, set apart from the bustle of the main street. The food is Canarian to inter-national – and, if you like, they can come up with a roast or a schnitzel to make any guest feel at home.

✠ 194 C1 ✉ Peatonal La Chalana 4
☎ 928 167 166 ⊕ www.lafaroladelmar.net
🕐 Daily 5pm–11pm

La Cofradía €–€€

From the outside, this restaurant on the harbour wall looks rather like a wooden cabin. Inside, it has a cosy maritime atmosphere. Anyone who wants the freshest of fish at a moderate price will find what they are looking for from all the catches hauled onto the harbour mole.

✛ 194 C1
✉ Muelle Pesquero s/n ☎ 928 166 447
🕐 Daily 9am–midnight

Coronado €€–€€€

This evening restaurant in the apartment complex of the same name has been among the best in town for years. You can spend a very pleasant evening here in elegant surroundings; the wonderful Spanish and international cuisine is complemented by an excellent selection of wines. The prices here are accordingly somewhat higher than elsewhere. All dishes are very attractively presented. There are a few tables outside near the swimming pool.

✛ 194 C1
✉ Calle El Sol 14 ☎ 928 541 174
🌐 www.restaurantecoronado.com
🕐 Tue–Sat 5:30–11:30

San Borondon II €–€€

This bodega is located slightly above the string of restaurants on the front, in the heart of the old part of the town. Try the small tapas dishes here with a glass of house wine or sangria.

✛ 194 C1
✉ Plaza Cirilo López 1 ☎ 928 541 428
🕐 Daily 11am–1am

Where to… Shop

JANDÍA PLAYA

Most of the south's shopping opportunities are confined to the shopping centres of Jandía Playa and Costa Calma. However, there are also other shops here selling perfume, jewellery and souvenirs, in addition to the supermarkets. The oldest shopping complex is the Centro Comercial Cosmo on the through road (Avenida del Saladar).

A weekly market is held next door every Thursday from 9am to 2pm. It has a wide selection of clothes and souvenirs but also a lot of cheap items and kitsch.

COSTA CALMA

The El Palmeral shopping centre on the main road in Costa Calma, next to the petrol station, has a number of different boutiques. Light summer fashions made of natural materials can be found at Earth Collection; 1st One stocks costume jewellery and gemstones.

Centro Comercial Costa Calma is another shopping centre that also has a supermarket with a wide range of products.

MORRO JABLE

The old part of Morro Jable only has a few shops of interest. Off the square that has several cafés, bars and restaurants, is Fuerte Cabrito on the Calle Nuestra Señora del Carmen.

LA LAJITA OASIS PARK

The shop at La Lajita Oasis Park sells a wide range of home accessories and unusual gifts. There is also one of the island's largest garden centres in Oasis which also sells small plants that can be carried in your hand luggage. You don't need an entrance ticket to access the shop.

Where to… Go Out

NIGHTLIFE

Most of the nightlife in this part of the island is confined to the large hotels and resort club complexes.

The liveliest spots are still to be found in Jandía Playa – such as in the Bar Oasis (Avenida del Saladar 5) which mixes good cocktails.

The locals like to unwind as well.

In Morro Jable **El Navegante** (Calle San Juan 3) has a wonderful roof terrace that fills up mainly at the weekend – and then only after 11pm.

There is generally a good atmosphere next door in the **Bodega San Borondon II** which also serves good tapas (p. 126).

B-Side (p. 124) in the Bahía Calma Shopping Center is a good address in Costa Calma

WATER SPORTS

The **Pro Centre René Egli**, based at Sotavento Beach, is one of Europe's top centres for windsurfing. It is an excellent venue for just getting started or for polishing up your technique.

Organised dives and diving courses can be had with the English-speaking **Diving Center Werner Lau** (www.wernerlau.com). It is located in Jandía Playa in the Club Aldiana, but guests from elsewhere are also welcome.

The same applies to **Acuarios-Jandía** (www.acuarios-jandia.de/en/) in the Sotavento Beach Club in Costa Calma.

On the west coast, **La Pared** has become an El Dorado for surfers. Several schools there offer surf camps and expert tuition, for example **Waveguru** (tel: 619 804 447; www.waveguru.de) and **Adrenalin Surfschool** (tel: 928 949 034; www.adrenalin-surfschool.com).

OTHER SPORTS

Walking holidays on Fuerteventura are becoming increasingly popular and there are now many marked routes even on the Jandía isthmus. A particular favourite is the trail from Morro Jable via a mountain pass to Cofete. Near the lighthouse in the little village of El Puertito, a path leads to the cliffs of Caleta Madera or to Punta Pesebre. **Time for Nature** (tel: 928 872 545; www.timefornature.de) organises guided tours, also to other parts of the island and on Lobos.

Tennis Matchpoint (www.matchpoint-world.de/en) offers courses in hotel complexes on the Jandía peninsula (incl. Jandía Princess, Faro Jandía and Sotavento Beach Club).

EXCURSIONS

Yachts to charter, big-game fishing trips and catamaran excursions are available from the harbour in Morro Jable – the only one on Jandía peninsula. 4-hour sailing trips can also be booked, e.g. on the *Santa María*, when you can also watch delphins and whales (www.catamaran-santamaria.com).

A windsurfing and kiteboard school

A touch of the Orient – a caravan of camels against Lanzarote's fascinating volcanic landscape.

Lanzarote

Fuerteventura's smaller companion island is famous for its volcanic scenery and the attractions created by César Manrique.

Pages 128–157

Getting Your Bearings

Lanzarote covers a surface area that is half that of Fuerteventura. Nevertheless, there is lots to see on the neighbouring island. Magnificent volcanic scenery littered with black lava fields contrast with white fincas, often with a date palm or two, that provide a green highlight.

A good road from the ferry port of Playa Blanca allows visitors to reach the white village of Yaiza in next to no time. This is the gateway to Timanfaya National Park that gained its presence appearance in 1730–36 following a series of volcanic eruptions that buried eleven villages under rock and molten ash. Even today, the whole area gives the impression that the natural catastrophe only happened yesterday – burnt up and virtually without any vegetation, you feel you are on the moon.

South of the national park is Lanzarote's biggest resort, Puerto del Carmen. Like Corralejo it retains its original fishing port alongside a long beachfront, popular with tourists. To the east is Arrecife, the capital, with an interesting mix of old and new buildings.

Due north at Tahiche, built into volcanic caves, is the incredible former home of the island hero and driving force César Manrique. Just north of this is the old capital of Teguise, Lanzarote's historical *tour de force*, a beautifully preserved collection of houses and *palazzos* (palaces) which date back to the 15th century.

Isla
Graciosa

Órzola

34 Mirador
del Río

Cueva de
los Verdes

10 ★ ★
Jameos
del Agua

Haría **33**

Arrieta

La Caleta
de Famara

La Santa

Sóo

Mala

5 km

Tinajo

3 mi

Tiagua

Teguise
29

Guatiza

35 Jardín
de Cactus

9 ★ ★
Parque Nacional
Timanfaya

Fundación César
Manrique
32

Tahiche

San Bartolomé

Costa
Teguise

Ifo **30**

La Geria
31

Güime

Yaiza

Tías

36
Arrecife

La Hoya

Aeropuerto
de Arrecife

37
Puerto del
Carmen

Playa
Blanca

My Day
on Fuerteventura's smaller companion island

Considering that the ferry crossing only takes 30 minutes, an excursion to the neighbouring island is really a must. Unlike Fuerteventura, the volcanic past is that much more present on Lanzarote. A visit to Timanfaya National Park could well be the most outstanding highlight of your whole holiday. Be ready for a big surprise!

 **9am: A Picture-Postcard Village at the Foot of the Volcano**

From the ferry terminal in <u>Playa Blanca</u> a good road takes you to <u>Yaiza</u>. This large village on the edge of the national park boasts an architecture unique to Lanzarote – gleaming, white, cube-shaped house with added chimney stacks, the doors and window frames are painted a uniform green. As if by a miracle, the village was not damaged by the devastating volcanic eruptions in the 18th century. Eleven neighbouring villages, however, were buried under the lava, boulders and ash.

10am: Like Being on the Moon

On the approach to **9** ★★ <u>Timanfaya National Park</u> you may be lucky enough to encounter a caravan of camels crossing the road. Every morning, these undemanding

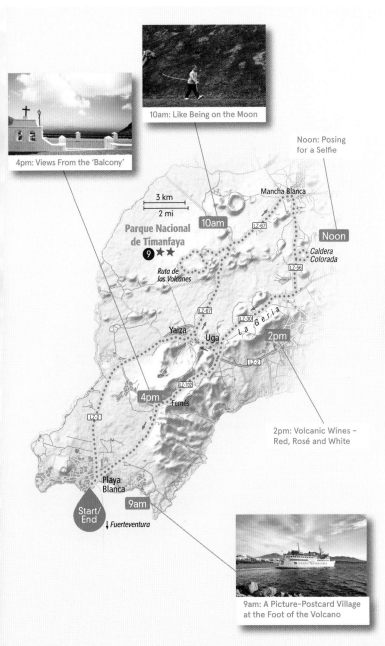

4pm: Views From the 'Balcony'

10am: Like Being on the Moon

Noon: Posing for a Selfie

3 km
2 mi

Mancha Blanca

Parque Nacional de Timanfaya
9 ★★

10am

LZ-67

Noon

Caldera Colorada

LZ-56

Ruta de los Volcanes

P

LZ-67

LZ-30

La Geria

Yaiza

Uga

2pm

LZ-2

4pm

LZ-702

Femés

2pm: Volcanic Wines –
Red, Rosé and White

LZ-2

Playa Blanca

9am

Start/End

↓ *Fuerteventura*

9am: A Picture-Postcard Village
at the Foot of the Volcano

Winegrowing on Lanzarote: Every vine grows in a small pit.

animals set off for Echadero de los Camellos ('Camel's resting place') where busloads of tourists wait to be able to take a short ride on the back of these ships of the desert.

On the big car park at the centre of this conservation area, a demonstration of the temperature just a few inches below the ground is given every few minutes to an amazed public. A park official pours water into a pipe and a few moments later a hissing and steaming 'geyser' shoots into the sky.

The extent of the historical natural catastrophe becomes obvious on a 30-min. coach trip around the <u>Ruta de los Volcanes</u>.

Even almost 300 years after the last series of eruptions, everything looks more or less as if it could have happened yesterday.

Noon: Posing for a Selfie

Excursions on your own are not allowed in the central area of the national park. However, just a little bit beyond the boundary of the park (on the LZ56 to the south of Mancha Blanca) you can stretch your legs along a volcanological trail. If you follow the circular path anti-clockwise around the Caldera Colorada, starting out from the walkers' car park, you will come to a magnificent volcanic bomb

10am

4pm

2pm

Top: The hissing fountain of water is an artificially made mini-volcano.
Above: Palm trees to either side of the whitewashed Church of San Isidro Labrador in Uga.
Right: Winegrowing on volcanic soil.

after about ten minutes walk that provides the perfect setting for a holiday selfie with the fiery-red slope of the volcanic cone in the background.

2pm: Volcanic Wines – Red, Rosé and White

Carry on down the LZ56 heading south until it meets the wine route from La Geria – an area covering 5,100 hectares (12,600 acres) that is geographically-speaking in the very centre of the island. And: surprise, surprise! The inhospitable volcanic plain suddenly turns into a landscape cultivated with small vines. Just a few years after the devastating volcanic eruptions, the farmers on Lanzarote had a

Above: One of many bodegas with its many barrels.

Right: The restaurant Casa Emiliano in Femés

sparkling idea – namely, to plant vineyards in the middle of the burnt out landscape. Each individual vine is in a funnel-shaped pit that is protected by a low, semicircular stone wall. Thousands of these combine to make a unique work of landscape art.

You can sample the volcanic wines in a bodegas along the road and perhaps buy one or other bottle – practical three-bottle packs are also available – to take back with you to Fuerteventura.

 4pm: Views From the 'Balcony'

The road from Uga via Femés is an alternative to taking the same

4pm

road back to <u>Yaiza</u>. The mountain village is famous for its view from the 'balcony of <u>Rubicón</u>'. From the church square – with the church of San Marcial de Rubicón (15th century) – you have a wonderful view over the Rubicón plain and the whole southern part of Lanzarote. On the horizon, the light-coloured sandy dunes of Corralejo can be made out.

Simply take a seat in one of the two eateries on the 'balcony', e.g. Casa Emiliano, and tuck into a snack or something more substantial. You have plenty of time as the ferry terminal in Playa Blanca is just a 20-minute drive from here.

❾ ★★ Parque Nacional de Timanfaya

Why	To feel you have been on the monn at least once in your lifetime.
Don't Miss	The picture-book volcanic scenery.
Time	Half a day.
What Else	You can take a short walk and see a huge volcanic bomb en route.
In Short	Lava, lava everywhere – a fascinating and unique place.

Hikers in a solidified lava gully

Born out of fire! It is not really surprising that the volcanic cones in Timanfaya are called 'fire mountains' (montañas del fuego), especially when you see them bathed in the late afternoon light. No trees, no bushes as far as you can see. Only burnt cinders and rough lava fields. Despite all this, a trip around this region that was declared a national park in 1954 is incredibly exhilarating.

The series of eruptions in the 18th century went on for six years. A bizarre landscape was created as a result with some

300 volcanic cones, the highest of which is Timanfaya at a height of 510m (1,673ft). The name commemorates the village of Timanfaya that, along with ten other villages, was consumed by lava and wiped off the map. As if by a miracle, nobody was killed. A slight earthquake preceded

the eruptions and, as eye-witnesses reported, there was a 'muffled rumbling', giving the inhabitants enough warning to get to a safe place in time.

Long considered an area that cannot be used for anything, this protected region covering some 5,100 hectares (12,600 acres)

The entrance to the Parque Nacional de Timanfaya

has since become Lanzarote's main tourist attraction. More than half a million visitors want to see this surreal natural spectacle every year and feel what it is like on another planet. The US American space authority, NASA, tested its moon buggy here for use on the Apollo missions.

On a Camel or a Bus

It is best to approach from the south; the volcanic debris begins just north of Yaiza and an impish César Manrique designed devil welcomes you to the park. It is forbidden to leave your vehicle and walk among the *malpais* (literally, badlands), unless supervised by a qualified guide, and the first parking point is at the Echadero de los Camellos ('Camel Park'). This can be a chaotic spot, though, as tour buses stop here to let off passengers who want to queue for dromedaries to take them on the short camel ride up and down the mountainside. It's worth a look but the most spectacular part of the park is still to come.

Once past the pay booth you must drive the short way into the park and leave your car next to the Visitor Centre. Here a park ranger demonstrates that the volcano beneath your feet is still very much alive; a bucket of water is emptied into a tube in the ground and transformed into a scalding geyser; a dry bush is dropped into a fissure and promptly ignites.

Also from here coaches depart more or less continuously on the Ruta de los Volcanes tour (Route of the Volcanoes; the price of the trip is included in the admission fee to the park). This is an unforgettable 35-minute trip, with a short commentary in different languages, taking in the highlights of the central part of the park, such as a lava tunnel and a lava lake or the Valle de la Tranquilidad ('Valley of Tranquility'), a small valley covered in layers of ash and fine-grained lapilli (little volcanic stones varying from the size of a pea to a walnut).

The only shame is that the bus doesn't stop anywhere so you have to take in (and photograph) this primeval landscape through the window of a bus.

A Volcanic Bomb on the Side of the Path

Lanzarote can offer magnificent volcanic scenery outside the national park as well. The area around the villages Mancha Blanca and Tinajo also suffered from the devastating eruptions in the 18th and 19th centuries. Unlike in the national park, you are free to explore this region at

The earth's natural geothermal heats this barbecue.

your leisure. You can stretch your legs on the educational volcanic walk at the foot of the Caldera Colorada. After walking for about ten minutes heading eastwards from the car park on the LZ56 to Mancha Blanca (at km 3.4), you will come across a volcanic bomb with a diameter of almost 4m (13ft). How did this massive boulder get here in the first place? Was it perhaps tossed through the air?

Inhabitants refer to this unforgettable stretch of countryside as the *Malpaís*, literally the 'badlands'

INSIDER TIP In the national park, the **Restaurant El Diablo** with its wide picture windows and unique volcanic barbecue in particular is a one-off – but the food is unfortunately second rate. You are better off going to one of the eateries in Yaiza, e.g. **Bodega de Santiago** where you sit in the shade of a wonderful rubber tree. The restaurant is on the northern edge of the village right on the road within the national park (tel: 928 836 204; www.labodegadesantiago.es).

✛ 196 B2/3
☎ 928 173 789
⊕ www.cactlanzarote.com

❶ Daily 9–5:45, Summer until 6:45, last coach tour 5/6pm
🎟 €10

❿ ★★ Jameos del Agua

Why	A volcanic natural wonder in a class of its own.
Time	Two to three hours.
When	Late afternoon is best when most of the coaches with day-trippers have left.
What Else	The Cueva de los Verdes – a second lava cave – is virtually next door.
In Short	One of the island's highlights.

A perfect symbiosis of nature, art and architecture! And certainly one of the masterpieces – if not *the* ultimate work – by Lanzarote's all-round talent, César Manrique.

With a sure eye for the unusual, the artist transformed a lava tunnel into one of the biggest tourist attractions on the Canary Islands. And the final touch to the overall work of art is a mini pool that has been inserted between the black basalt walls in the shade of the palm trees above. Swimming in it, however, is not allowed, nor

One of the *jameos* is now a pool in an idyllic setting

is it possible in the small subterranean lake, filled with sea-water, hidden under a lava roof.

The show caves on Lanzarote's north coast were formed when the volcano Monte Corona erupted some 3,000 years ago and a molten stream of lava found its way along a mile-long lava tunnel to the sea, where is continues under water for a little further. In the course of time, sections of the roof over the tunnel, that is only a few feet under the surface, collapsed. Such collapsed lava tunnels are known as *jameo* on Lanzarote – there are around 20 of them on the island, whereby the Jameos del Agua is the largest and by far the best known. Under César Manrique's management, the island's government commissioned the tunnel system – that was being used more or less as a rubbish tip – to be turned into a kind of fantasy cave landscape in the 1960s.

You descend into the first *jameo* to find a cool dark café-bar area, filled with lush tropical plants. New Age mood music may be playing. As your eyes adjust you can see little niches and alcoves that come into their own at night when it becomes

a restaurant – occasional musical events are staged here. This is joined to a cave with a lake. Peer closely and you will see that the still water is populated by hundreds of tiny almost fluorescent white spider-like albino crabs. They once lived deep in the ocean but were stranded here long ago and this is the only place in the world where they are now found.

Pool and Volcano Houses

When you emerge from the dark lake into daylight, you are in for another surprise! In the second *jameo,* Manrique inserted a gleaming blue pool between basalt walls. Surrounded by palm trees and with whitewashed rock, it conjures up images of a beach in the South Seas. Next to the pool is the entrance to an auditorium seating 600 that has been ingeniously integrated into the cave. This is an extraordinarily venue, not least of all due to its exceptional acoustics. Concerts and folkloric shows regularly take place here. From the pool, a flight of white steps leads up to the Casas de los Volcanes where, in addition to a research centre, an interactive exhibition is located where you can find out more about volcanism on Lanzarote and the other Canary Islands.

Greeen Cave

If you want to visit another impressive lava cave then head for the Cueva de los Verdes (The Green Cave) that belongs to the same subterranean cave system as Jameos del Agua.

The entrance is just a few miles away. It takes its name from a family who once lived here and in the 16th and 17th centuries was used by the islanders as a refuge from pirates and slave traders. Unlike the Jameos del Agua these huge caves, comprising several large halls, have been changed little apart from the lighting that skillfully picks out the rock formations. The guided tour lasts around 45 minutes and includes going down steps along sometimes narrow passageways to a depth of 53m (174ft) below the surface. At the end of the tour the guide has a surprise in store for you – but we won't spoil this by telling you!

The Cueva de los Verdes is just part of one long lava tunnel.

INSIDER TIP There are two restaurants in Jameos del Agua which are, however, both expensive. One alternative, is the fish restaurant **El Amanacer** (p. 155) in Arrieta. just five minutes drive away.

Jameos del Agua
✠ 197 F4 ⊕ www.cactlanzarote.com
🕐 Daily 10–6:30
🎫 €9.50; Evening events (dinner and music; Tue, Sat, in summer also Wed) 7:30–0:30 ca. €40

Cueva de los Verdes
✠ 197 E/F4
⊕ www.cactlanzarote.com
🕐 Daily 10–5 (Guided tours every hour on the hour)
🎫 €9.50

㉙ Teguise

Why	Colonial flair like in the late Middle Ages.
Time	Half a day.
When	If you want to explore the streets on your own, come here during the week as there is a market on Sundays which attracts lots of people.
What Else	A wonderful view can be had from the castle on its exposed hilltop.
In Short	A beautifully preserved historical town.

A stark contrast to the modern holiday resorts on the coasts! Teguise has retained something of the flair of the colonial era and, at first glance, would appear to have changed little since the arrival of the Spaniards more than 600 years ago. The Old Town with its grand houses, old monasteries and invitingly peaceful squares is beautifully presented and is now virtually all preserved as a site of historic interest. A number of boutiques invite visitors to stop by and there is no lack of good restaurants and street cafés either.

The popular market takes place every Sunday.

The kitchen in the Museum Palacio Spínola.

Founded in 1406, Teguise is one of the oldest settlements on the Canary Islands. It served as the island's capital until 1852 before passing this function on to the up-and-coming harbour town of Arrecife. Unlike the latter, Teguise has not been spoilt by districts of featureless new buildings. Instead, it has retained its historical town centre in its entirety. Small and easy to explore, it only takes 15 minutes to walk from one end to the other with lots of things to discover on the way in the sometimes generously laid out squares and narrow alleyways.

For six days of the week Teguise slumbers, but on Sunday thousands of visitors flock here to its touristy market, which takes over the town centre. Folklore dancers and musicians perform on the Plaza de la Constitución. The main square is dominated by the handsome Iglesia de Nuestra Señora de Guadalupe, the foundation of which date back to the 15th century. However, the interior, damaged by a fire in 1909, was poorly restored and is disappointing.

On the square you can visit the Palacio Spínola, built from 1730–80, now the Timple Museum (casa-museo) that focuses on the music and culture of the Canary Islands. You can also look inside the Caja Canarias bank (closed on Sunday), which was once the cilla or church grain store, built in 1680.

Next to the main square the Plaza de Julio 18 is lined with historic buildings now home to shops and restaurants. Just off the square there is a very picturesque snowy white-topped building with a characteristic Canarian balcony. This is the 17th-century Casa Cuartel, formerly an army barracks.

Sacred Art

One of the town's two convents has also found a new role. The 18th-century Convento de Santo Domingo houses modern art exhibitions, while the handsome 16th-century Convento de San Francisco is now a museum of sacred art (Museo Diocesano de Arte Sacro), displaying altarpieces and liturgical items. Have a look up at the wonderfully fashioned coffered ceiling executed in the Mudéjar style.

Don't miss the Palacio del Marqués, once the seat of the island's government. In the 19th century it was the home of the aristocratic Herrera y Rojas family which turned the house into the island's cultural centre. The margravial town palace originally occupied a whole block; what now remains is an attractive building with an intimate courtyard where you can enjoy a glass of wine and soak in the colonial flair.

The Castle on the Hill

The best view of the old capital and the volcanoes that rise up in the distance can be had from the Castillo de Santa Barbara. The castle sits at the top of the Montaña de Guanapay. A little road leads up to the fortress (16th century). A pirate museum has been set up within the old walls – not something you definitely have to have seen! It's the view that counts.

INSIDER TIP You are spoiled for choice: The **Bodega Santa Barbara** (Calle Cruz 5; tel: 928 845 200 is particularly good or opt for the **La Cantina** (p. 155).

✛ 197 D3

Oficina de Turismo
✉ Pl. de la Constitución
☎ 928 845 398
🌐 www.turismoteguise.com

**Convento de San Francisco/
Museo Diocesano de Arte Sacro**
✉ Pl. de San Francisco
🕐 Tue–Sat 9:30–4:30, Sun 10–2
💶 €2

**Palacio Spínola
(Casa-Museo del Timple)**
✉ Pl. de la Constitución
☎ 928 845 181 🌐 www.casadeltimple.org
🕐 Mon–Sat 9–4 (9–3 in summer),
Sun 9–3 💶 €3

**Castillo de Santa Bárbara/
Museo de la Piratería**
☎ 928 59 48 02
🌐 www.museodelapirateria.com
🕐 Daily 10–4

Almost Swallowed Up

When approaching El Golfo it looks like a completely normal volcano with rugged flanks and a jagged crater rim. When seen from the other side the full impact of what must have been an incredible natural spectacle can be seen. The south side of the volcano has slipped completely into the sea. At the foot of the crater wall with wonderful contrasting colours, varying from ochre to rust-red, is an emerald-green lagoon, separated from the deep blue of the Atlantic by a black sandbank.

At Your Leisure

30 El Golfo
Next to the little white fishing village of El Golfo is one of the island's most curious coastal and volcanic landscapes. Arriving from the south there are two approaches. The first is signposted 'Charco de los Clicos' and takes you past a remarkably eroded and striated cliff to a black lava beach and a spectacular rock outcrop. At the back of the beach, half of the El Golfo volcano has fallen away to create an amphitheatre rich in reds and orange hues. The star sight is the enclosed lagoon, which has a deep emerald green colour, probably caused by algae, though another theory is that it may also be due to the presence of the semi-precious stone olivine.

The best view of the lagoon is actually from above, on the elevated walkway accessed from the village (follow the signpost to El Golfo).

✛196 B2

The rugged rock formations at El Golfo

31 La Geria
Lanzarote's wine-growing region is like no other in the world. Vines are planted in pits so that they can delve deep beneath the layer of volcanic ash down to the soil. Each is surrounded by a horseshoe-shaped dry stone wall, about a metre high, which helps the lava covering the crop to retain what little moisture there is and protects it from the wind. The sight of thousands of these *zocos*, as they are known, against the dark lava landscape is quite stunning.

The very best in the wine-growing area can be found on the LZ30 between Uga and the Monumento al Campesino. Extensive vineyards and lots of *bodegas* offering wine tasting lie along the narrow road. El Grifo, one of the market leaders, also has a wine museum and an adjoining cactus garden (www. elgrifo.com; daily 10:30–6, until 7 in summer).

✛196 C2

32 Fundación César Manrique (El Taro de Tahiche)
The Fundación César Manrique promotes artistic environmental and cultural activities and was created by the great man himself in 1982. It is based at the remarkable home of Manrique called Taro de Tahiche. Like Jameos del Agua

(p. 142), which it pre-dates, it is built on the site of a lava flow – several of the extravagantly furnished rooms are underground. It houses a contemporary art collection, including many works by Manrique, but the star exhibit is the dwelling itself.

✠ 197 D2
✉ Tahiche ☎ 928 843 138
🌐 www.fcmanrique.org
🕐 Daily 10–6 💶 €8

33 Haría

This charming little pristine town of white cube-like houses sits in the beautiful 'Valley of 1000 Palms' and inevitably invites comparison with a North African oasis. Haría is a magnet for the art and crafts community and has some very good shops. During the week visitors can look inside the craft centre Tienda y Taller de Artesanía Municipal, where several basket weavers and embroiderers have their workshops. A craft market is held every Saturday on the Plaza León y Castillo (Haría Artesanal; Sat 10–2:30). The town's main attraction is the Casa-Museo César Manrique – Manrique's former home where the artist spent the last few years of his life. It lies in a shady palm grove on the southern edge of the town, just a few minutes walk from the main square. During opening hours you can also have a look inside the artist's studio where – as in the house itself – nothing has been changed since his sudden death in 1992 as the result of an

The pretty little town of Haría is peacefully located in the 'Valley of a Thousand Palms', surrounded by a number of impressive volcanoes.

accident. His simple grave is in the local cemetery on the edge of town on the road to Arrieta.

✚ 197 E4

Tienda y Taller de Artesanía
✉ Calle El Puente s/n
🕐 Mon–Sat 10–1, Tue–Sat 3:30–6:30
🐾 Free

Casa-Museo César Manrique
✉ Calle Elvira Sanchez 30
☎ 928 843 138 🌐 www.fcmanrique.org
🕐 Daily 10:30–6 🐾 €10

34 Mirador del Río

A *mirador* is a lookout point and this one, originally a gun battery, is probably the most spectacular in the whole archipelago. It was carefully designed by César Manrique so that neither the entrance nor the curving corridor which takes you into the main room give you any idea what is coming next – which is a wide-angle almost aerial view through full-length windows of the Isla la Graciosa and the bright blue straits of El Río. You can go outside to appreciate the *mirador*'s location, set into the side of a jaw-dropping sheer cliff face that plummets 450m (1476ft) to the sea.

✚ 197 E5 🌐 www.cactlanzarote.com
🕐 Daily 10–5:45 🐾 €4.75

35 Jardín de Cactus

Even if you are not a garden fan you will probably be fascinated by this one. César Manrique's last bigger project, created on the site of a former quarry, was opened in 1990. Once again he demonstrated that he was not just a talented painter and architect but also an exceptional landscape gardener who knew how to show the prickly plants off to their best advantage. The collection now comprises some 4,500 plants and 450 different species from all over the world. Remarkable simply because of their size are the towering Mexican saguaros and a group of golden barrel cactii ('mother-in-law's cushions'); flourishing Canary Island spurge and other sub-tropical succulents in all shapes and sizes grow alongside each other. An old, restored *gofio* mill at the top of the site has become the cactus garden's symbol. From here, you have a lovely view over the garden, laid out like an amphitheatre. Beyond the garden walls there are extensive fields of prickly pears (opuntia). Cochineal insects were bred in large numbers in the 19th century on the ear-shaped segments

A prickly afternoon out at the Jardín de Cactus.

Evening on Arrecife harbour where not only cruise liners and ferries lie at anchor but also fishing and rowing boats.

of this cactus. The red dye derived from these insects was once a popular natural product for dying cloth and, to a lesser extent today, is used as a colouring in the foodstuff industry. Up until just a few years ago, cochineal gave Campari its characteristic colour.

> ✚ 197 E3
> ✉ Between Guatiza and Mala
> ☎ 928 529 397
> 🌐 www.centrosturisticos.com
> ⏱ Daily 10–6 (last admission 5:45)
> 💰 €5.80

36 Arrecife

People only used to come to the capital of the island on rainy days to go shopping. The local council has, however, made a big effort to turn it into a more attractive place.

In the meantime, there are a number of sights – for the galleries and museums alone you will need to plan at least half a day. The most recent project is a new marina with a modern shopping centre and a chic row of restaurants and cafés. The harbour basin in Puerto Naos, slightly to the north was enlarged and cruise liners now stop by regularly. A footpath from the seaside promenade over the Puente de las Bolas takes you to Castillo de San Gabriel, a moated fort built by the Italian engineer Leonardo Torriani around 1590 on a little island slightly separated from the mainland. A small museum on the island's chequered history is now housed in the somewhat claustrophobic rooms inside the mighty fortress walls. Don't miss going up onto the roof of the building from where there is a panoramic view over the capital to the surrounding volcanoes. In front of the fortress a rusty cannon points exactly at the only high-rise building on Lanzarote – now a luxury hotel with a skyline restaurant (p. 155). For the island's greatest artist, César Manrique, it was however the island's biggest eyesore that he would have loved to have blown to pieces!

Take a stroll along the pedestrianised shopping street and turn off to find the picturesque Iglesia de San Ginés, beautifully restored to its 18th-century glory. Behind here the Charco (lagoon) of San Ginés is a peaceful spot for a walk, with its fishing boats at anchor and choice of bars and restaurants around the lagoon.

Further on, a short walk just past the port, is the capital's main visitor attraction, the Castillo de San José, built in the late 18th century and restored by César Manrique to hold the internationally acclaimed Museo Internacional de Arte Contemporáneo (International Museum of Contemporary Art). Mostly modern Canarian art is presented in the vault-like rooms. The dark painted walls lend the works a unique character of their own. Exhibits also include works by the painters Óscar Domínguez and Pepe Dámaso of Gran Canaria. César Manrique is of course represented with several of his works. The fort also houses a good restaurant (p. 154), designed according to an idea by Manrique. In the area of low water between the fort and the quay where the cruisers lie at anchor there are a number of concrete equestrian figures in the water that catch everyone's attention – an installation called *Rising Tide* with which the British artist Jason deCaires Taylor takes a stand against climate change.

✢ 197 D2

Castillo de San Gabriel/ Museo de Historia de Arrecife
☎ 928 802 884
🕐 Mon–Fri 10–5, Sat 10–2 💰 €3

Castillo de San José/ Museo Internacional de Arte Contemporáneo (MIAC)
✉ Carretera de Puerto Naos
☎ 928 812 321 🌐 www.cactlanzarote.com
🕐 Daily 10–8 💰 €4

37 Puerto del Carmen

Puerto del Carmen is Lanzarote's main resort. Its main strip, the Avenida de las Playas, is lined with scores of bars, restaurants and nightspots and its beaches stretch half way to Arrecife. There are more than enough shops and eating options here to keep you happy. The most attractive part of the town is around the port.

✢ 196 C2

Where to... Eat and Drink

Expect to pay for a meal for one, excluding drinks

€   under €15
€€   €15–€25
€€€   over €25

PUERTO DEL CARMEN

La Cofradía de Pescadores La Tiñosa €€
This restaurant on the harbour wall run by the fishing cooperative always serves fresh fish caught that day. The fish platter is very opulent and includes everything brought in on the fishing boats.

✝ 196 C2
✉ Plaza del Varadero
☎ 660 433 578 🕐 noon–11

La Casa del Parmigiana €€
This elegant trattoria is especially popular even though its terrace is next to Farione's sports centre and it has no view worth mentioning. Reservation recommended. The pizza and home-made pasta dishes almost taste like those made in Italy and the Tuscan wines do so anyway.

✝ 196 C2
✉ Calle Alegranza 1
☎ 928 512 731
🌐 www.lacasadelparmigiano.es
🕐 Daily 1–11:30

La Lonja €–€€
Located in the old town district directly by the harbour, La Lonja used to be Puerto del Carmen's fish market, today it is a lively restaurant. In the usually well frequented bar on the ground floor, you can drink a beer or a glass of local wine as you nibble on a tapa, or savour a piece of fish in the main restaurant.

✝ 196 C1
✉ Calle Varadero s/n
☎ 928 511 377
🕐 Daily noon–midnight

ARRECIFE

Qué Muac €€
After enjoying the artworks in the Castillo de San José, try out the restaurant built to a design by César Manrique – an elegant room with wooden floorboards and black plastic chairs in the 1960s style, not

Lag-O-Mar: a magical cave-like setting surrounded by lava and palm trees.

What better place to eat freshly caught fish than in a fish restaurant located right on the sea?

forgetting the panoramic picture window with a lovely view over the harbour basin and the cruise liners. The modern Canarian food is creative as well, serving cress soup with sweet potatoes or tasty kid served on a light banana purée.

🕂 197 D2
✉ Carretera de Puerto Naos
(in Castillo de San José ☎ 928 812 321
🌐 www.cactlanzarote.com
🕓 Tue-Thu noon-4, Fri, Sat noon-4, 7-11
(bar 10am-midnight)

Star City €€

If you want to be above everything else, then head for the Café-Bar Star City at the top of Lanzarote's only high-rise. A glass lift next to the reception in the Arrecife Gran Hotel takes visitors to the 17th floor. For a 5-star hotel, the coffee and snacks are not over-expensive. And the view over the capital and the Playa del Reducto from 75m (246 ft) up is worth it, too.

🕂 197 D2
✉ Parque Islas Canarias s/n
(in Arrecife Gran Hotel) ☎ 928 800 000
🌐 www.aghotelspa.com
🕓 Daily 9:30-midnight

TEGUISE

La Cantina €€-€€€

This rustic restaurant on the fringe of the Old Town has a good selection of tapas in addition to burgers and steaks accompanied by Canarian beer and a cup of fair trade coffee. Very popular; reservations recommended.

🕂 197 D3 ✉ Calle León y Castillo 8
☎ 928 845 536 🌐 www.cantinateguise.com
🕓 Daily 10-11

Lag-O-Mar €€

This restaurant, one of the most unusual on the island, is tucked away just 2km (1¼mi) to the south of Teguise in the residential area Nazaret. It has a spectacular location in a former quarry and is part of a villa that is now a museum. It once belonged to the film star Omar Sharif for a short time although he never actually lived here himself. Enjoy the Mediterranean food served at tables arranged around a pool in the shade of palm trees.

🕂 197 D3 ✉ C/Los Loros, 2, Nazaret
☎ 928 845 665 🌐 www.lag-o-mar.com
🕓 Tue-Sat noon-midnight, Sun noon-6

The restaurant in the Casa Museo del Campesino is surrounded by other buildings in the traditional style of the island with whitewashed walls and green shutters.

ARRIETA

El Amanacer €€
If you are lucky, you will find a spot on the terrace overlooking the sea. This popular restaurant has a large selection of fresh fish and seafood dishes. The *cherne* (sea bass) is always good and – like the other fish dishes – is served in the classic fashion with Canarian potatoes and a *mojo* sauce.
✛ 197 E4 ✉ Calle La Garita 46
☎ 928 835 484
🕐 Fri–Wed noon–8

YAIZA

La Era €€€
The country house restaurant on the edge of Yaiza is well known on the island. It is housed in a farmhouse from the 17th century that was stylishly restored by César Manrique and opened in 1970. Several cosily furnished dining rooms open off a large central courtyard. Just as typically Canarian as the location is the Canarian cuisine that – unfortunately – doesn't quite come up to the same standard as its wonderful atmosphere.
✛ 197 E4
✉ Calle El Barranco ☎ 928 830 016
🌐 www.laera.com 🕐 Tue–Sun 1–11

LA GERIA

Bodega El Chupadero €–€€
This restaurant in the middle of a wine-growing area is situated slightly above the road (LZ30) and can be reached along a short unmade track. The reward is a wonderful view over the glinting green vineyards. Delicious small dishes are served to accompany the wine in peaceful surroundings. The freshly made tomato soup or the smoked salmon from Uga are always a good bet.
✛ 196 C2 ✉ La Geria
☎ 928 173 115 🕐 Tue–Sun noon–9

MOZAGA

Casa Museo del Campesino Restaurante €€–€€€
Almost every trip around the island takes you past the Monumento al Campesino (monument to the peasant farmers) that can be seen from miles around. It was – of course – designed by César Manrique, as was the res-

taurant next to it. Typically Canarian food is served in this rustic *bodega*. A huge dining room one floor down is used for larger events.
✝ 197 D3 ✉ San Bartolomé
☎ 928 520 136 🕐 Daily noon–4

HARÍA

El Cortijo €€€
This 200-year-old farmhouse has been beautifully restored. Sit inside the dark cosy rooms or on the large sunny terrace. Suckling pig, roast lamb, rabbit with rosemary and grilled meats are the specials.
✝ 197 D3 ✉ El Palmeral
☎ 928 835 686 🕐 Daily noon–9

Where to... Shop

PUERTO DEL CARMEN

The Biosfera Plaza, a ten-minute walk uphill from the port, is the best shopping centre in town. Spread over four floors, it is home to international fashion outlets, souvenir shops and restaurants. Unusual crafted items and fashion jewellery can be found at Arteguise (Planta/level 1). A Spar supermarket is useful for self-catering holiday-makers (Planta/level 3). The shopping centre is located on the Avenida Juan Carlos I and is open from Monday to Saturday from 10am until 10pm and on Sunday from 11am until 9pm.

Chévere on the Avenida de las Playas (near the Centro Aquarium) stocks a good selection of olivine and lava stone jewellery. Wholemeal bread and organic vegetables from the island are available in the small but well-assorted organic shop in the Centro de Terapia Antroposófica (Calle Salinas 12).

ARRECIFE

The pedestrianised centre includes a wide range of shops that appeal to both islanders and visitors. The main street is Calle León y Castillo and you will find most of the main shops on or just off here. There are plenty of local stylish clothes and accessories shops too.

A market (Mercado Turístico y Artesanal) selling handicrafts and food is held every Sunday from 9am until 2pm on the Plaza de Las Palmas outside the parish church of San Ginés.

The largest shopping centre on the island is Disland on the dual carriageway from Arrecife to the airport with some 60 different shops, restaurants and cinemas (exit: Playa Honda; Mon–Sat 10–10, Sun and holidays 11–9).

TEGUISE

Teguise, the island's original capital, is famous for its Sunday market (p. 145). The shops in the narrow lanes in the Old Town are not outlets of international fashion labels but privately owned small boutiques and shops. The Artesanía Lanzaroteña on the Plaza de Constitución is the best address for textiles and souvenirs from Lanzarote.

It is worth popping into the Emporium (Calle Notas 15; www.emporium.es) just to admire its original setting. The former cinema now showcases oriental furniture. Home accessories, jewellery, porcelain and decorative fabrics, most of which are imports from China and Tibet.

A good address in the holiday resort Costa Teguise is Pueblo Marinero, another creation of the artist César Manrique. A craft fair (Paseo Artesanal) is held here every Wednesday from 6pm until 10pm where you can keep an eye out for fashion jewellery, homemade soap and leather items.

HARÍA

A market (Mercado de Artesanía) selling local products and handicrafts is held every Saturday from 10am until 2.30pm on the Plaza León y Castillo in Palm Valley in Haria.

Bread and groceries are available during the week in the little market hall (Mercado Municipal de Abastos).

Pottery, cactus jam and all sorts of souvenirs can be found in El Palmeral de Dulce next to the restaurant El Cortijo.

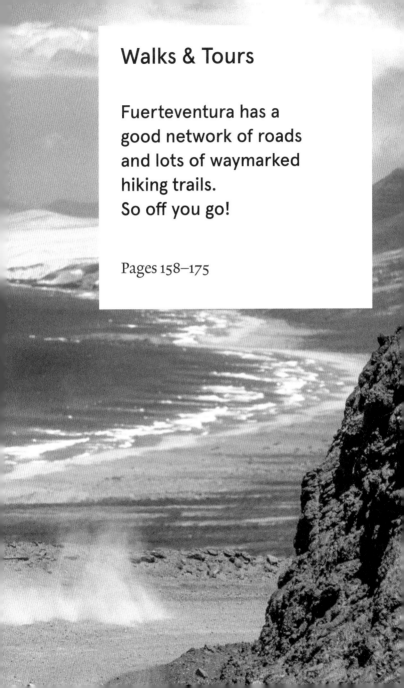

Walks & Tours

Fuerteventura has a good network of roads and lots of waymarked hiking trails.
So off you go!

Pages 158–175

Isla de Lobos

What	Walk
Distance	10km (6mi)
Time	3hrs
Start/End	El Muelle (the harbour) ✠ 191 E5

You will feel like a desert island explorer here. Lobos (p. 48) is a microcosm of 'the mainland' with mini-volcanoes, small lagoons, a superb little beach, a tiny ramshackle fishing village, a picturesque lighthouse and mountaintop views that equal any on Fuerteventura. Choose a clear day to enjoy it. You need a modicum of fitness to climb the mountain; while boots are not necessary, sturdy trainers are a minimum requirement. See p. 48 for more on the island.

There is never much activity in the tiny fishermen's settlement of El Puertito.

Getting to the Starting Point

Several small ferry boats depart for Lobos from the harbour in Corralejo every day. The crossing takes just 20 minutes. The first leaves at 10am, the last boat back is at 4pm. Apart from a very basic place to eat (food only available if booked in advance) there is no infrastructure of any sort on the island. Make sure you take enough drinking water with you and something to eat. There is little shade on the island so you will need a sunscreen and a hat.

1–2

Close to the jetty there is a small kiosk with information on the flora and fauna of this tiny island. Head off to the right in the direction of Las Lagunitas. After a few minutes walk you will reach El Puertito ('the little port'). This uninhabited settlement comprises a few cobbled-together huts and small

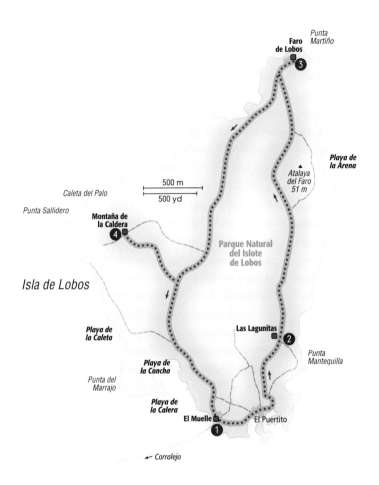

stone buildings where the fishermen store their equipment.
Walk through it and fork right to head to the sea. The path
is well marked, and anyway the island is too small to get
lost. At the edge of a small promontory you look out across
to Lanzarote. To your right is Las Lagunitas ('the little
lagoons'), a sandy salt marsh where migratory birds come
to feed and rest.

View of the Isla de Lobos.

2–3

As you reach the end of the salt flats the path turns right towards the sea but this is no more than a short detour. Ignore it and keep going straight ahead following the trail up a slight incline to the left where it leads to what appears to be a small white tin shelter. In fact, as you get closer this turns out to be the back of an information board on the flora and fauna of Las Lagunitas. Look across the island and you can see right back to the dunes of Corralejo. A broad sandy path leads from here to the Faro de Lobos (lighthouse) and should take you another 25 to 30 minutes.

Just before you reach the Faro at Punta Martiño, the northernmost part of the island, you pass by a number of small brown protuberances, typically around 10–15m (33–50ft) high. These are *hornitos* (literally 'little ovens'), mini-volcanoes, formed not in the usual way, by magma pushing up the earth, but by steam-driven explosions (known technically as phreatic eruptions) that occur when water beneath the ground is heated by magma, lava, hot rocks or new volcanic activity. These were created some 8,000 years ago and are best appreciated from the lighthouse. From here there are also tremendous views across to Lanzarote and Playa Blanca: to the east of the holiday resort on Lanzarote you can make out the light-coloured, famous sandy beaches of Papagayo glittering in the sun with the hotel complexes in Puerto del Carmen a little bit further north. From the lighthouse in the northern-most corner of Lobos, a wide path continues back southwards.

3–4

Continue on the broad sandy path for around 15 minutes. The Montaña de la Caldera looms large to your right but avoid the temptation to take the first turn off to the right, which in fact leads to Caleta del Palo. Take the next path right – 'Montaña de la Caldera 30 mins'. This refers to the time it takes to reach the 127m-high (416ft) summit. This is quite a steep climb so take it easy, particularly as the steps finish about three-quarters of the way up and the last part is a bit of a scramble. It's well worth the effort, however. The 360-degree views covering the three islands of Fuerteventura, Lanzarote and Lobos itself are exhilarating.

The excursion boats and catamarans anchored off the white-sand bay to your left are a picture, while way down below, on the other side of the ridge, is the almost perfect semicircular stone beach of Caleta del Palo.

It used to be possible to walk along the relatively wide crater rim from the summit to another viewpoint. This is, however, now prohibited in order to protect the natural environment.

4–5

Descend the mountain and return to the main track. Turn right and it's a five-minute walk to the lovely little white sand crescent of Playa la Concha. This is an ideal spot for family bathing, with very calm waters and a gently sloping sandy bottom. From here, it is just a few minutes walk to the harbour to catch the boat back to Fuerteventura.

INSIDER TIP The only place to eat on the island is the very basic **Chiringuito Lobos** in El Puertito. If you want to eat something, you must order either on the boat or immediately on arrival. The choice is limited to fried fish and paella.

Sendero de Bayuyo

What	Walk
Distance	5km/3mi
Time	2hrs–2hrs 30mins
Start/End	Just north of Lajares ✛191 D4

A view of the Montaña Colorada with its deep holes.

The Sendero de Bayuyo was the first of what is now a well-developed network of marked hiking trails. It takes you past dramatic volcanic formations and offers wonderful views to the north of the island and beyond.

To find the start of the walk, take the FV109 to Lajares from Corralejo. Just before Lajares, opposite the Witchcraft Surf Shop (on the left), look to your right and you will see a curious purple-brown volcano with two depressions – this is where you are heading! To get there continue for 500m to the football ground (bus stop) and turn right just in front of it. Continue for another 1,000m

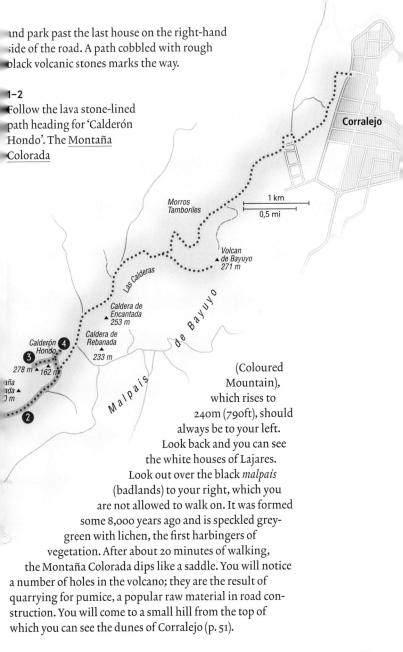

and park past the last house on the right-hand side of the road. A path cobbled with rough black volcanic stones marks the way.

1–2

Follow the lava stone-lined path heading for 'Calderón Hondo'. The <u>Montaña Colorada</u>

Corralejo

Morros Tamboriles

1 km
0,5 mi

Volcan de Bayuyo
▲ 271 m

Las Calderas

Caldera de Encantada
▲ 253 m

de Bayuyo

Caldera de Rebanada
▲ 233 m

Calderón Hondo
❸ 278 m ▲ 162 m

❹

aña ada ▲ 0 m

❷

Malpaís

(Coloured Mountain), which rises to 240m (790ft), should always be to your left. Look back and you can see the white houses of Lajares. Look out over the black *malpaís* (badlands) to your right, which you are not allowed to walk on. It was formed some 8,000 years ago and is speckled grey-green with lichen, the first harbingers of vegetation. After about 20 minutes of walking, the Montaña Colorada dips like a saddle. You will notice a number of holes in the volcano; they are the result of quarrying for pumice, a popular raw material in road construction. You will come to a small hill from the top of which you can see the dunes of Corralejo (p. 51).

2–3

After around 30 minutes you will pass through a drystone wall. Due north on the horizon is Lanzarote. After another five to ten minutes the path forks. Go left. After three to four minutes of steep climbing you will reach a viewing platform on the Calderón Hondo crater rim at an altitude of 230m (755ft). This not only offers a wonderful panorama but also lets you peer right down into the extinct crater of the volcano. Look to your left and you will see a 'cowl' that shows how the volcano collapsed. Down in the crater prickly pears are growing. You can skirt part of the crater lip but it is not

Once back in Lajeres or Corralejo again you can regain your strength in one of the restaurants.

recommended to try to walk right around it. The panorama in front of you stretches from the fishing village of Majanicho to the west to Puerto del Carmen on Lanzarote to the east. Some 3km (2mi) northeast is the 271m (889ft)-high Bayuyo volcano.

3–4

Descend the path and take the second fork left to the goat herders' building that you could see from the top of Calderón Hondo. Look inside this primitive shelter (it is a replica purpose-built for visitors) and you will see its thatch and mud roof construction set on volcanic drystone walls. The small conical construction nearby shows how a primitive oven was fashioned.

4–1

At this point you can head back the way you came or explore the volcanoes. Use Bayuyo as your guide point, and in an hour or so you will be standing below it. If you want to climb the summit it takes around 30 minutes and offers wonderful views. Corralejo is another hour or so walk away.

INSIDER TIP ▶ Remember to take plenty of water with you. There are several good places in Lajares for lunch (p. 64/65).

Highlights in North and Central Fuerteventura

What	Drive
Distance	151km/94mi (with options for short cuts)
Time	Full day
Start/End	Corralejo (from the roundabout by the football ground) ✙ 191 E5

This full-day drive will show you the best of north and central Fuerteventura. The good roads and relatively few cars means that driving is easy. Nevertheless, due to the number of things to see on the way, it is advisable not to set out too late. If you want to visit one or other of the museums, don't plan your excursion on a Sunday or Monday.

1–2

Begin in Corralejo. At the roundabout next to the football pitch on the western outskirts, turn off onto the new main road (FV 1) in the direction of Puerto del Rosario. To the right is the massive Volcan de Bayuyo, that rises to a height of 271m (889ft). It was formed some 30,000 years ago and, together with its neighbour to the east, is responsible for the Malpaís de Bayuyo badlands, a barren lava field, that

Peering through the flowers: Tindaya, the holy mountain.

extended the surface area of the island quite a bit to the north.

After about 8km (5mi) south of Corralejo turn off towards Lajares and, if you have time, make a detour to El Cotillo (p. 58) on the northwest coast. From the Torre del Tostón, a pirate's lookout on the edge of the cliffs dating from the 18th century, you can look across the Playa del Castillo, a favourite among surfers. To the north of the old fishing port there is a narrow road that leads to the lighthouses on the Punta del Tostón in the northwestern corner of the island.

3–4

On returning to Lajares, head south to the former capital La Oliva (p. 55). None of the olive trees that gave the place

its name exist any more. Instead, aloe vera is now being cultivated and can be seen as you enter the town. A soothing gel sold in many places on Fuerteventura is produced from its leaves and makes a perfect souvenir for those looking for something

The Ecomuseo de la Alcogida is located in the south of Tefía.

typical from the island. The centre of La Oliva is dominated by the church tower made of dark dressed stone. The fortified Casa de los Coroneles on the southern edge of the town highlights how important this little town once was. The building was the seat of the military governors who exercised their power with a strict hand.

Carry on along the FV 10 from La Oliva. After 5km (3mi) Montaña de Tindaya (p. 60), that was considered a holy place by the indigenous inhabitants of the island, appears ahead of you. Another 2–3km (1½–2mi) further on, the 366m (1,200ft) high Montaña Quemada can be seen on the right.

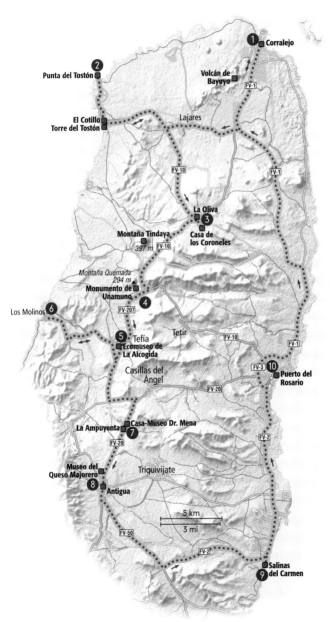

① Corralejo

② Punta del Tostón

Volcán de
Bayuyo

FV-1

Lajares

El Cotillo
Torre del Tostón

FV-10

FV-1

La Oliva

③

Montaña Tindaya
397 m
FV-10

Casa de
los Coroneles

Montaña Quemada
294 m
Monumento de
Unamuno

④

FV-207

⑥ Los Molinos

Tetir

⑤ Tefía
Ecomuseo de
La Alcogida

FV-10

FV-3

⑩

Casillas del
Ángel

FV-1

Puerto del
Rosario

FV-20

La Ampuyenta

Casa-Museo Dr. Mena

⑦

FV-20

Triquivijate

FV-2

Museo del
Queso Majorero

⑧ Antigua

5 km

3 mi

FV-50

FV-2

Salinas
del Carmen

⑨

A larger-than-lifesize figure at its foot commemorates the Spanish poet and philosopher Miguel de Unamuno.

4-6

Turn right off the main road onto the FV207 shortly after the Unamuno statue towards Puerto del Rosario. The road crosses a largely uninhabited plain where the fields have now been abandoned. A windmill serves as a reminder that grain was once grown and flour for *gofio* made here.

The well-presented open-air museum Ecomuseo de La Alcogida (p. 84) in the small village of Tefía shows how people lived here in simple conditions well into the 21st century.

A detour to the west coast after leaving Tefía is certainly worthwhile. A good side road leads to the tiny fishing village Los Molinos (p. 89). Most of the simple cottages, built around a bay with black sand, are occupied only at the weekends. A footbridge across the mouth of the Barranco de los Molinos provides access to a minute fishermen's chapel on the black beach. The generally large waves here are not very inviting to those who want to swim. Instead, you can sit on the terrace of the very simple café-bar overlooking the bay.

6-8

South of Tefía the road divides. If you turn right, you will reach Betancuria (p. 78) in the mountains. If you turn left towards Puerto del Rosario and right after 5km (3mi), you will come to the FV20 – the most important route from Puerto del Rosario across the centre of the island. 2km (1.2mi) further on, in La Ampuyenta, stop for a visit to the Casa-Museo Dr. Mena (irregular opening times). Diagonally opposite, a well restored red and white building stands out. Erected in 1891, it was intended to be a hospital but was never used as such.

South of La Ampuyenta are the windmills of Antigua (p. 82). The first of these, located right on the road and forming part of the Museo del Queso Majorero (p. 83), can also be visited inside. There is also a delightful, small botanical garden here too with tall saguaros, Canary Island spurge and other exotic plants that all thrive in Fuerteventura's dry island climate.

8-10

Almost in the centre of Antigua, turn off the FV 20 to the left onto the FV 50 that meets the FV2 about 10km (6mi) further on which takes you to the <u>Salinas del Carmen</u> (p. 90) in the tiny village of <u>Las Salinas</u>. Sea salt was once harvested in the salt evaporation ponds that have since been declared an historic industrial monument. You can found out more in the Salt Museum. The salt pans, laid out like a chess board, can also be seen from outside. The fish restaurant Los Caracolitos (p. 95) above the beach in the hamlet Las Salinas is an inviting place for a break before continuing your journey.

On the east coast, head northwards. After passing the airport, you bypass <u>Puerto del Rosario</u> (p. 86). Visit the island's capital another time: you will need to plan at least half a day. To the north of Puerto del Rosario you rejoin the new main road back to <u>Corralejo</u>.

INSIDERTIP It will probably be too early in the day to have lunch in El Cotillo but you should stop at least for a cup of coffee in one of the cafés on the old harbour. Otherwise, **Los Podomorfos** (p. 65) at the foot of Montaña Tindaya on the outskirts of Tindaya is a lovely place to sit or in the fish restaurant **Los Caracolitos** (p. 95) in Las Salinas where the tables are right on the water's edge.

A very popular photo motif is the isolated chapel La Virgen de la Peña, consecrated to the island's patron saint.

Coast-to-Coast

What	Walk
Distance	10km (6mi)
Time	Around 3hrs
Start/End	Centro Commercial El Palmeral, Costa Calma ✛195 D3

It is not difficult to walk from one side of Fuerteventura to the other – especially on the Istmo de la Pared. At this point the island is just 5km (3mi) wide and, if you begin your hike from the shopping centre El Palmeral, it is even less. The other side of the isthmus is completely undeveloped with romantic cliffs shaped by the wind and waves.

1–2

El Palmeral shopping centre is the perfect starting point. It is located on the through road from Costa Calma, next to the petrol station. Pass to the right (east) of the complex and take the narrow one-way street, Calle de la Playa de la Jaqueta until you get to the dual carriageway. The sandy path starts on the other side of the road. To reach the underpass turn right and walk some 400m parallel to the road and then the same distance back again on the other side.

Costa Calma is one of the tourist strongholds, but you can still find quiet spots.

The sandy track which is closed to traffic takes you past the Parque Eólico Cañada de la Barca. The 45 modern turbines on this wind farm make an important contribution to providing the island with sustainable energy.

2–3
Many parallel tracks cross the island at this point but simply follow your nose as they all head due west. This is a popular walk so you will rarely be on your own. Away to your right (the north west) the hills and low mountains

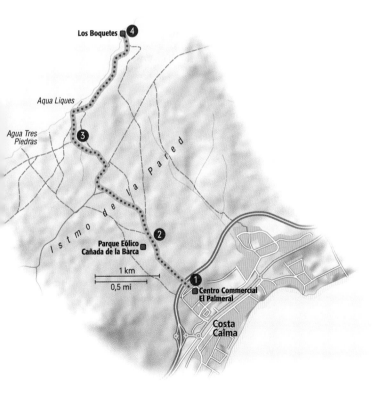

A large wind park generates much needed electricity.

often sit broodily. The sandy path rises almost unnoticeably and takes you through an area virtually devoid of vegetation. One plant, the thorny dwarf bush *Launaea arborescens* is only found outside the Canary Islands on the northwest coast of Africa. Another, the so-called false sowthistle (*Reichardia tingitana*) which has pretty yellow daisy-like flowers, is also originally from Africa. Little sand dunes are continuously created here by the trade winds.

3–4

The west coast is reached in about an hour after crossing the intersection with the hiking trail GR131 – a long-distance path over 153km (95mi) from Corralejo in the north to the Punta de Jandía, the most southwesterly point on the island. Step down carefully to the beach and look at the weird eroded shapes that have been caused in the alternating layers of basalt and fossilised sand. It may not be apparent to the human eye, but at the base of this escarpment there are natural springs that provide a welcome watering hole for birds such as the houbara bustard.

Continue to the northeast along the narrow ledge close to the water's surface: the eroded shapes become more spectacular. A huge sand dune slopes right down to the beach. A little further north black lava outflows provide

The *Chlamydotis undulata* is one of the rarest birds on the island.

rock pools for paddling. The power of the sea is demonstrated by the large waves which create a spectacular show by breaking off the rocks high into the air. You cannot swim here – the waves are much too big almost the whole year round and there are dangerous undercurrents.

Hike along the edge of the water until you reach <u>Los Boquetes</u> – a large dark cliff that stops you going any further. This is a truly romantic spot. Soak in the view of this wild stretch of coastline before heading back home again.

4–1

From here you can either return the way you came, which is the easiest option or climb up the large sand dune following a sandy track and cross the isthmus on one of the paths heading in-land. The hotel complexes in <u>Costa Calma</u> cannot be missed.

INSIDER TIP Don't do this walk if it is exceptionally windy as you risk being sandblasted and half-blinded by dust and sand. Take plenty of water with you as there are no shops along the path. There are a number of simple snack bars in **El Palmeral** Shopping Centre for you to choose from, either before or after your walk.

Practicalities

This is where you'll find important information prior to your trip, such as the best means of travel and other tips.

Pages 176–188

The quay in Puerto del Rosario is a popular meeting place.

BEFORE YOU GO

Advance Information
Websites
www.holaislascanarias.com
The Canarian government's official 'Welcome website' provides a short introduction to all the Canarian islands.

www.visitfuerteventura.es
The site operated by Fuerteventura's tourist authority provides lots of information on things to explore on the island.

www.artesaniaymuseosdefuerteventura.org
A museum guide with up-to-date opening times.

www.spain.info
Online information on the Canary Islands is also available on the Spanish tourist authority's website. Other sites worth a look are **www.fuertenews.com**, an English-language weekly magazine and their offshoot island guide.

Spanish Tourist Offices
UK
6th floor, 64 North Row,
W1K 7DE London
Tel: +44 020 73 17 20 11
www.spain.info/en_GB

Ireland
Callaghan House, 13–16 Dame Street,
D02 HX67 Dublin
Tel: +353 016 350 200
www.spain.info/en

Canada
2 Bloor Street West, Suite 3402,
4W 3E2 Toronto-Ontario
Tel: +1-416-961-4079
www.spain.info/en

USA
60 East 42nd Street, Suite 5300 (53rd Floor),
New York, NY 10165-0039
Tel: +1-212-265-8822
www.spain.info/en_US/

Concessions
Discounts are available for the over 60s on flights and ferries between the different Canary Islands. There are no discounts for students.

Consulates and Embassies
British Consulate
Calle Luis Morote, 6–3°,
35007 Las Palmas, Islas Canarias, Spain
Tel: +34 928 262 508
www.gov.uk/world

U. S. Consulate
Edificio ARCA,
C/ Los Martínez Escobar 3,
Oficina 7, 35007 Las Palmas, Islas Canarias, Spain
Tel: +34 928 271 259
https://es.usembassy.gov

Consulate of Ireland
Calle León y Castillo, 195,
35004 Las Palmas, Islas Canarias, Spain
Tel: +34 928 297 728
www.dfa.ie/irish-embassy/spain

Embassy of Australia
Torre Espacio, Paseo de la Castellana, 259D,
28046 Madrid, Spain
Tel: +34 913 536 600
https://spain.embassy.gov.au

Canadian Embassy
Torre Espacio, Paseo de la Castellana, 259D 28046 Madrid, Spain
Tel: +34 913 828 400
www.canadainternational.gc.ca/spain-espagne

Currency and Foreign Exchange
As in the rest of Spain, the Canary Islands have adopted the euro. Notes are in denominations of 5, 10, 20, 50, 100, 200, 500; coins come in 1, 2, 5, 10, 20 and 50 cents and 1 and 2 euros.
Major **credit cards** are widely accepted in the resorts, but don't rely on these elsewhere.

Customs

Since the Canary Islands enjoy a special status, there are strict limits on the amount of goods that can be exported for personal use. The allowances to other EU countries are one litre of spirits, two litres of wine and either 200 cigarettes or 50 cigars. All food, plants, animals, and related products must be declared. When returning home, make sure that you are aware of the regulations of your customs authority.

Electricity

The power supply is 220–225 volts. Sockets take standard continental-style plugs with two round pins. Visitors from the UK require an adaptor (often available at the airport). Visitors from the USA will require a voltage transformer.

Health

Insurance Citizens of EU countries receive reduced-cost emergency health care with relevant documentation (European Health Insurance Card), but private medical in-surance is still advised and essential for all other visitors.

The Hospital General de Fuerteventura (Carretera del Aeropuerto Km 1; tel: 928 862 000) is the place to contact in the event of accidents or serious illnesses. Outpatient treatment available in all major tourist centres. For addresses contact your hotel reception or your respective con-sulate/embassy (p. 178).

Drugs Outside opening hours a sign on the door of a pharmacy gives the address of the nearest one open. Medicine is generally cheaper in Spain than in many other European countries.

National Holidays

1 Jan	New Year's Day
6 Jan	Epiphany
28 Feb	Andalucían Day (regional)
March/April	Easter Monday
1 May	Labour Day
30 May	Día de Canarias (Day of the Canary Islands)
15 Aug	Assumption of the Virgin
12 Oct	National Day
1 Nov	All Saints' Day
6 Dec	Constitution Day
8 Dec	Feast of the Inmaculate Conception
25 Dec	Christmas Day

Personal Safety

Break-ins in apartment blocks and cars are relatively common in the larger holiday resorts of Corralejo and on the Jandía peninsula. Hotel rooms in all major centres have safes (for which a charge is generally made).

Staying in Touch

Post: A postcard to the UK or northern Europe will usually take about 7–12 days. The state post offices are generally open from Mon–Fri 9am–2pm, Sat 9am–1pm. Beside the state-run postal service *Correos*, there are also private service providers on the Canaries with their own stamps (*sellos*) and letterboxes. It is therefore important to make sure you use the right letter box when you send your postcards. State letter boxes are yellow and often have a slot marked *extranjeros* for mail abroad.

Telephones: Mobile/cell phones (*móvil*) will automatically choose the appropriate partner network when you arrive. Since 2017 roaming charges are not due under a safeguard (fair use) limit. Fuerteventura's network is very well developed.

International Dialling Codes

Dial 00 followed by:

UK	44
USA/Canada	1
Ireland	353
Australia	61
New Zealand	64

Emergency Numbers

Police (Policía Nacional)	☎ 112
Fire (Bomberos)	☎ 112
Ambulance (Ambulancia)	☎ 112

Internet Access

Many hotels provide Wi-Fi for their guests, but the service is not always free of charge. You can usually surf free of charge in many cafés and restaurants. Look at the entrance for the 'WiFi' sign and, where applicable, ask for the password (*clave, contraseña*).

Time

Unlike the rest of Spain, the Canary Islands observe Greenwich Mean Time (GMT). Summer time (GMT+1) operates from the last Sunday in March to the last Sunday in October

Travel Documents

Travellers need a passport. National driving licences and motor vehicle registration certificates are recognised. Dogs and cats travelling from the EU need an EU Pet Passport as well as a microchip with their identification number. At least 30 days need to have passed since the rabies vaccination, and not more than a year.

If your pet is travelling from outside the EU, for example USA, Canada, or Australia, the same rules apply as above, and a licensed vet must also complete a non-commercial EU health certificate for the Canary Islands within ten days of your travel date.

When to Go

Fuerteventura's well-balanced climate means that it is an all-year-round travel destination, and even in the coolest months of the year in January and February you can still bathe in the sea. The peak season is the winter, especially Christmas, but the Easter period is also very popular.

GETTING THERE

By Air

There are numerous charter flights throughout the year from London and other European cities. Most seats are sold by tour operators as part of a package holiday, but it is possible to buy a flight-only deal though travel agents or on the internet. For independent travellers, the disadvantage of charter flights is that you are usually restricted to a period of 14 days.

The Spanish national airline, **Iberia**, operates regular scheduled flights to Fuerteventura, but these are expensive and unless you are already living in Spain they are not worth considering.

From the airport to the holiday resorts: bus no. 3 runs approx. every 30 mins. to Puerto del Rosario from where there are connections to Corralejo and Caleta de Fuste. Bus no. 1 also runs every half-an-hour to resorts on the Jandía peninsula. Buses run less frequently on Sundays and on public holidays.

By Sea

The ferry company **Trasmediterránea** has a weekly car ferry service from Cádiz on the Spanish mainland to Tenerife and Gran Canaria. The journey from Cádiz to Las Palmas takes around 50 hours (www.trasmediterranea.es/en). The crossing is relatively expensive and only of interest to those spending a long time on the islands and cannot be without their own car.

GETTING AROUND

Buses

Island buses (*guaguas*) travel to most places on Fuerteventura. **Tiadhe** (www.tiadhe.com) offers a dense network of buses between the main towns, but there are few to no buses to the smaller and more remote places. Timetables are available at the large bus stations and tourist offices. The buses are very punctual.

Taxis

Taxi drivers are obliged to switch the **taxi-meter** on. The trip from the airport to Puerto del Rosario costs about 12 euros, and to Morro Jable about 95 euros.

Driving, Car Hire

Compared with prices in Central Europe, car hire rates on Fuerteventura are quite reasonable. Depending on the supplier and the hire time, you pay between 20 and 30 euros a day for basic models. Owing to the lower taxation on petrol here, **filling** up is also much cheaper than on the mainland. Regardless of whether you book from home, at one of the international car hire companies or at a local rental company on Fuerteventura, mileage is never limited. The **major car hire companies** (Avis, Europcar, Hertz...) have offices at the airport, but lots of local companies (the largest is Cicar, www.cicar.com), have offices directly in the arrival hall. Find out what is included in the insurance cover and how high your excess is in the case of damage. One of the few providers who offer full insurance without excess is Sunny Cars (www.sunnycars.de). As the driver you have to be at least 21 years old and in possession of a credit card.

The **roads** are in a good to very good condition. As the population density is relatively low there are seldom any hold-ups. Parking spaces are rather in short supply in the holiday resorts Corralejo, Morro Jable and Caleta de Fuste, in particular.

Speed limits are 90kph (56mph) on the open road, 100kph on dual carriageways and motorways, and 40kph (25mph) in urban areas. Drive on the **right-hand side** of the road. Vehicles coming from the right have priority. On roundabouts, vehicles already on the roundabout always have right of way.

The legal **alcohol limit** is 50mg alcohol per 100ml blood. Fines, especially for speeding, are very high in Spain and collection agencies make sure that they are paid, even from abroad.

Boat

Excursions taking several hours along the south coast of Fuerteventura are available from the harbour in Morro Jable. One boat trip not to be missed is from Corralejo to the island of Lobos (p. 48).

Boats **shuttle** to and from the neighbouring island every day. The crossing takes 20 minutes (www.navieranortour.com). The **ferry** from Playa Blanca to Corralejo

(Fuerteventura) does not need much longer; business is shared between the Naviera Armas (www.naviera-armas.com) and Fred Olsen (www.fredolsen.es) shipping companies.

If you want wheels on Lanzarote, then arrange for your hire car to be brought to the Playa Blanca. Most hire companies will not allow cars to be taken from one island to another. One exception is the Canarian company Cicar (www.cicar.com), as long as the car is brought back to the island on which it was hired.

Island Hopping

First-time visitors to the Canary islands can fit in two or three islands on one holiday. Many tour operators offer holidays on more than one island. You can depend on a very good network of **flight and ferry connections**. Lanzarote makes a very nice **day trip** (see p. 130).

A fast ferry runs three times a day to Las Palmas de Gran Canaria (www.fredolsen.es) from Morro Jable (journey time: 120 minutes). If you take the earliest ferry you will have enough time to stroll around the largest and most interesting town in the archipelago and even visit the spectacular aquarium in Las Palmas harbour.

It is best to travel to the other Canary Islands by air; the Iberia subsidiary Binter flies several times a day to Gran Canaria and Tenerife, from which there are connecting flights to La Palma, La Gomera and El Hierro (www.bintercanarias.com).

ACCOMMODATION

From a middle-class hotel to a luxury resort with a pool, there is an enormous choice of hotels, apartment complexes and holiday homes.

Most people book a package deal through a travel agent, opting for just breakfast, half-board or all-inclusive. Self-caterers and individual travellers, who wish to organise their holiday independently can find lots of accommodation options on Internet portals (e.g. www.booking.com). As long as you don't need the beach on your doorstep, plenty of pretty country hotels and fincas await further inland. Regardless of whether you want a package or individual solution, make sure you book in good time if you wish to go during the peak season in winter (especially over Christmas).

Prices

Expect to pay per double room, per night (breakfast not included):

€	under €60
€€	€60–€90
€€€	€90–€120
€€€€	over €120

FOOD AND DRINK

Classic Canarian cuisine may not become your favourite food – it is hearty country--style cooking, based on what the land and waters provide – but it is part of the cultural experience and you should give it a try.

You can find Canarian food in many country restaurants, while in the tourist centres you will find that the cuisine tends to be of a more Spanish and international character. As yet, Lanzarote cannot boast any star-studded gourmet restaurants, but the island does have a large selection of good hotel and excursion restaurants.

Prices

Expect to pay for a main course, excluding drinks and service:

€	under €15
€€	€15–€25
€€€	over €25

Regional Fish and Meat Dishes

Hearty soups and casseroles are an essential part of Canarian cooking. *Sancocho* and *zarzuela*, both hearty fish stews, have earned a certain acclaim. Meat and fish are generally *a la plancha*, grilled, and served with *papas arrugadas*, potatoes in a salt crust, and a *mojo picón* or *moja verde* sauce. Green *mojo* accompanies fish and red *mojo* meat. Atlantic fish include *vieja* (parrot fish) and *cherne* (stonebass); the white meat of the *alfonsiño* (sea perch) is also very good. Almost all meat is imported; besides beef steaks and pork chops, you will also find lamb and marinated rabbit on the menu; goat meat does tend to be from the island. The Canarian side dish *gofio*, a flour made from ground and toasted barley, maize or wheat, used to be a staple food even at the time of the Guanches.

Café solo, Carajillo, Sangria & Co.

Coffee culture on the islands has developed in the same way as the Canarian cuisine. While just 10–15 years ago, it was difficult to get anything other than the traditional *café solo* (the Spanish espresso) and the *café con leche* (milk coffee), Cappuccino and Latte macchiato are now matter of course. Barraquito (an expresso layered with condensed milk and frothy milk and carajillo (espresso with a shot of brandy) are another two of the Spanish-Canarian coffee variations on offer.

Wine is not grown on Fuerteventura itself but on the neighbouring islands, primarily Lanzarote and Tenerife. Lanzarote's best-known wine comes from the La Geria region; this wine together with the produce of the smaller wine-growing areas in San Bartolomé, Tinajo and Haría, bears a protected *Denominación de Origen*, designation of origin. Among the market leaders are the El Grifo and La Geria *bodegas*, both of which press acceptable table wines which can be found on the menus in many restaurants. Wine connoisseurs, however, usually opt for the imports from the Spanish mainland. The sangria though tastes good almost everywhere.

The locals often prefer to drink a fresh **draft beer** with their meal. The local brands are Tropical (from Gran Canaria) and Dorada (from Tenerife), and you order either a *caña* (small glass) or a *jarra* (big glass). Of course imported beer is also available.

Mealtimes and Tipping

People generally eat later than in Central Europe. Lunchtime is from around 1pm and dinner from 9pm. Hotels and tourist restaurants have adapted to the needs of their guests however and serve dinner from 7pm. Many places offer a good value *menú del día*: It consists of three very average courses with bread and a drink. **VAT and service** are included in the price, but a small **tip** of around 5% is still expected. It is important to remember that you do not round up the amount when paying or give the tip directly to the waiter or waitress. Leave the tip on the plate on which you received the change.

ENTERTAINMENT

Information on what to do on Fuerteventura, fiestas and cultural and sporting events (such as the windsurfing championship) can be obtained locally in tourist information offices or, of course, on the Internet, for example on the informative website www.whatsoninfuerteventura.com.

Nightlife

Music bars and discos can be found especially in **Corralejo** on the Avenida Nuestra Señora del Carmen, for example. Established and popular venues include Rock Café (in the La Plaza Shopping Center) and Waikiki Beach Club (Avenida Hernández Morán 11). There is always something going on every evening at the Plaza Feliz Estévez ('music plaza'). If you would rather party with the locals there are a few clubs with names that change from time to time in **Puerto del Rosario. Ask at the tourist information office for addresses.** Nightlife is otherwise largely limited to hotel bars.

Classical and Modern

High-end cultural events are few and far between on Fuerteventura.
One highlight is the **International Music Festival of the Canary Islands** in January and February (www.festivaldecanarias.com). This series of classical concerts is held in collaboration with the neighbouring islands, venues on Fuerteventura including the Palacio de Congresos in Puerto del Rosario and the parish church in Antigua.

Sports

Las Playitas Resort (www.playitas.net) on the east coast is a good address for sports enthusiasts who want to play golf or tennis or cycle. The Aldiana and Robinson clubs on the Jandía peninsula are well adapted to the needs of those who enjoy sports of all kinds. In the holiday resorts on the coast, almost everything naturally focuses on **water sports**. Here you can **swim**, **snorkel** and go out on **boat excursions**.
In the north, the best places to **dive** are in the straits between Corralejo and Lobos. The water around the Jandía peninsula is also good for sports enthusiasts. Excellent conditions for windsurfing and kiteboarding can be found on the Playa Barca and the beaches of Corralejo. Classical surfers are attracted more to the coast around La Pared.
Out of the water, **hiking** through the bizarre volcanic landscape has evolved into a popular pastime on Fuerteventura. The network of paths is not as well established as on the islands of Tenerife and La Palma that have specialised in hiking. However, there are a number of attractive way-marked routes.
Cyclists find ideal conditions here as there is very little traffic on many of the country roads away from the coast. Mountainbikes, racing bikes and more recently electric bikes can be rented in the larger centres.
Golf players have a choice between four 18-hole courses in Caleta de Fuste (tel: 928 160 034; www.fuerteventuragolf club. com and tel: 928 877 271; www.salinsasgolf. com), Jandía Playa (tel: 928 871 979; www. jandiagolf.com) and Las Playitas (tel: 828 860 400; www.playitas.net). Beginners can book introductory courses there too and several of the large hotels offers special packages for golf players.

SHOPPING

Fuerteventura is not really a shopper's paradise. However, if you have a bit of time you can find a number of lovely souvenirs, even in the holiday resorts. Local handicrafts, in particular, have experienced a huge boom thanks to the stream of tourists.

Low Tax Rate
Compared with other European countries, including the Spanish mainland, VAT is very low. The sum passed on to the customer varies tremendously from one shop to another. Alcoholic drinks and cigarettes, however, are generally cheaper. You also get a better rate for perfume and cosmetics.

Shopping areas
The biggest range of shops is to be found in Corralejo and Jandía Playa, but still choice is limited. As well as Canarian crafts (see below), there are dozens of surf shops (usually very expensive); perfumeries and jewellers both offering duty-free prices; and electronics shops selling watches, cameras and high-tech goods. The latter are invariably run by Asian traders and prices are almost always negotiable.

Where to shop?
In the tourist centres, there are *Centros comerciales* (shopping centres) on almost every corner, and there you will find supermarkets, boutiques and restaurants all under one roof. The offer is mainly focused on the requirements of the tourists. The **supermarkets** in particular often only have a limited range of products. One of the largest shopping centres on the island is Las Rotondas (www.lasrotondascentrocomercial.com) in Puerto del Rosario. This is where the locals buy their food and everyday things.
The **handicraft markets** held in in Corralejo (Tue and Fri), Morro Jable (Thu) and near the Oasis Park in La Lajita (Sun) are of interest. Here you can discover attractive souvenirs between the bric-a-brac and kitsch.

Canarian Classics
Typical souvenirs are culinary objects. Top of the list: a little glass of *mojo sauce*, a package of *gofio* or a jar of the cactus jam produced on the island. You can even take vacuum-packed **goat's cheese** on the plane, one of the best comes from the Quesería Maxorata and is available in many supermarkets. You can buy skin care products and other **aloe vera products** made from the medicinal plant that is now cultivated on Fuerteventura, directly from the aloe vera farm in Tiscamanita (on the FV30).
Craft articles are very popular and they can be found on the markets and in many boutiques and souvenir shops. These include **earthenware**, **wickerwork** and **handicraft**, as well as **fashion jewellery**. Handicrafts guaranteed to have been made on Fuerteventura can be found in the state-operated shops in the Museo del Queso (Antigua) and in the craft shop in the Mirador Morro Velosa.

Opening times
Most shops are open Monday to Friday from around 9–1 and 4–8 (Saturdays from 9–2). It is only in the tourist centres that the shops open all day without a lunchtime break, often staying open until 10pm and also opening on Sat and Sun.

EVENTS CALENDAR

Colourful, unusual and noisy celebrations are held all over Fuerteventura. And there are more than enough reasons to hold one – from folkloric village festivals to honour the local patron saint to carnivals with a South American touch.

January/February
Cabalgata de Los Reyes
Cavalcade of the Magi (Parade of the Three Wise Men) on 5–6 January in Puerto del Rosario.

Festival de Música de Canarias
A big classical music festival organised in collaboration with the neighbouring islands.

Carnaval

Highlights of the street carnivals are in Puerto del Rosario the selection of the carnival queen, the Regata de Achipenco (a weird and wonderful boat race) and The Burial of the Sardine (El Entierro de la Sardina) on Ash Wednesday.

April

A large agricultural fair (FEAGA) with a folkloric programme of accompanying events is held in Pozo Negro.

May/June
Corpus Christi

Celebrations are held all over the island but the finest sights are in Puerto del Rosario, where beautiful flower-patterned carpets are created on the streets.

Fiesta Nuestra Señora del Tanquita

At the end of May/beginning of June a pilgrimage takes place in Cardón to the cave chapel on Montaña Cardón.

July
Fiesta de San Buenaventura

In Betancuria the anniversary of the island's invasion by the Spanish crown is marked on 14 July.

Fiestas de la Virgen del Carmen

Homage is paid to the patron saint of fishermen in many coastal towns on 16 July.

Windsurfing and Kiteboarding
World Cup

In the second half of July the world's best professionals descend on the Playa Barca.

September
Romería Virgen de la Peña

Large pilgrimage in mid September in Vega de Río Palmas to honour the patron saint.

November

Fiesta Internacional de Cometas

Generally in the first half of November stunt kites fill the sky over the beach of Corralejo.

December

Rancho de Pascua

Nativity plays are held on Christmas Eve in Tiscamanita and Antigua.

Insider Tipp
Perhaps you would like to visit the neighbouring island Gran Canaria (✛ 198 C3) quickly as well, in addition to Fuerteventura and Lanzarote. There are several regular flights to La Palmas (tel: 902 391 392; www.binternet.com). Ferries to Las Palmas also run from Morro Jable that have the added advantage of arriving at the (more centrally located) port. The crossing takes around two hours. Apart from shops, cafés and restaurants the island's many sights include the Casa Colón, the Museo Canario, the Catedral de Santa Ana and the lively Mercado de Vegueta.

USEFUL WORDS AND PHRASES

Spanish (*español*), also known as Castilian (*castellano*) to distinguish it from other tongues spoken in Spain, is the language of the Canary Islands. The islanders' version has a sing-song quality more reminiscent of the Spanish spoken in Latin America than the mainland.

Ticket (single/return)	Billete (de ida/de ida y vuelta)
I'm lost	Me he perdido
Where is...?	¿Dónde está...?
How do I get to...?	¿Cómo llego a...?
the beach	la playa
the telephone	el teléfono
the toilets	los servicios
Left/right	Izquierda/derecha
Straight on	Todo recto

Greetings and Common Words

Do you speak English?	¿Habla inglés?
I don't understand	No entiendo
I don't speak Spanish	No hablo español
Yes/no	Sí/no
OK	Vale/de acuerdo
Please	Por favor
Thank you (very much)	(Muchas) gracias
You're welcome	De nada
Hello/goodbye	Hola/adiós
Good morning	Buenos días
Good afternoon/evening	Buenas tardes
Good night	Buenas noches
How are you?	¿Qué tal?
Excuse me	Perdón
How much is this?	¿Cuánto vale?
I'd like...	Quisiera/me gustaría

Emergency!

Help!	¡Socorro!/¡Ayuda!
Could you help me please?	¿Podría ayudarme por favor?
Could you call a doctor please?	¿Podría llamar a un médico por favor?

Directions and Travelling

Aeroplane	Avión
Airport	Aeropuerto
Car	Coche
Boat	Barco
Bus	Autobús/guagua
Bus stop	Parada de autobús
Station	Estación

Accommodation

Do you have a single/double room available?	¿Tiene una habitación individual/doble?
With/without bath/toilet/shower	Con/sin baño/lavabo/ducha
Does that include breakfast?	¿Incluye el desayuno?
Could I see the room?	¿Puedo ver la habitación?
I'll take this room	Cojo esta habitación
One night	Una noche
Key	Llave
Lift	Ascensor
Sea views	Vistas al mar

Days

Today	Hoy
Tomorrow	Mañana
Yesterday	Ayer
Later	Más tarde
This week	Esta semana
Monday	Lunes
Tuesday	Martes
Wednesday	Miércoles
Thursday	Jueves
Friday	Viernes
Saturday	Sábado
Sunday	Domingo

Numbers

0	cero
1	una/uno
2	dos
3	tres

4	**cuatro**
5	**cinco**
6	**seis**
7	**siete**
8	**ocho**
9	**nueve**
10	**diez**
11	**once**
12	**doce**
13	**trece**
14	**catorce**
15	**quince**
16	**dieciséis**
17	**diecisiete**
18	**dieciocho**
19	**diecinueve**
20	**veinte**
21	**veintiuno**
22	**veintidós**
30	**treinta**
40	**cuarenta**
50	**cincuenta**
60	**sesenta**
70	**setenta**
80	**ochenta**
90	**noventa**
100	**cien**
101	**ciento uno**
110	**ciento y diez**
120	**ciento y veinte**
200	**doscientos**
300	**trescientos**
400	**cuatrocientos**
500	**quinientos**
600	**seiscientos**
700	**setecientos**
800	**ochocientos**
900	**novecientos**
1,000	**mil**
5,000	**cinco mil**

Restaurant

I'd like to book a table	**Quisiera reservar una mesa**
A table for two please	**Una mesa para dos, por favor**
Could we see the menu, please?	**¿Nos trae la carta, por favor?**
What's this?	**¿Qué es esto?**
A bottle/ glass of...	**Una botella/ copa de...**

Could I have the bill please?	**¿La cuenta, por favor?**
Service charge included	**Servicio incluido**
Waiter/waitress	**Camarero/a**
Breakfast	**Desayuno**
Lunch	**Almuerzo**
Dinner	**Cena**
Menu	**La carta**

Menu Reader

a la plancha	grilled
aceite	oil
aceituna	olive
agua	water
ajo	garlic
almendra	almond
anchoas	anchovies
arroz	rice
atún	tuna
bacalao	cod
berenjena	aubergines
bistec	steak
bocadillo	sandwich
café	coffee
calamares	squid
cangrejo	crab
carne	meat
cebolla	onion
cerdo	pork
cerezas	cherries
cerveza	beer
champiñones	mushrooms
chocolate	chocolate
chorizo	spicy sausage
chuleta	chop
conejo	rabbit
cordero	lamb
crema	cream
crudo	raw
cubierto(s)	cover (cutlery)
cuchara	spoon
cuchillo	knife
embutidos	sausages
ensalada	salad
entrante	starter
espárragos	asparagus
filete	fillet
flan	crème caramel
frambuesa	raspberry
fresa	strawberry
frito	fried

fruta	fruit	pepino	cucumber
galleta	biscuit	pera	pear
gambas	prawns	perejil	parsley
gazpacho andaluz	gazpacho (cold soup)	pescado	fish
guisantes	peas	pez espada	swordfish
habas	broad beans	picante	hot/spicy
helado	ice cream	pimientos	red/green peppers
hígado	liver	piña	pineapple
huevos fritos/	fried/	plátano	banana
revueltos	scrambled eggs	plato principal	main course
jamón serrano	ham (cured)	pollo	chicken
jamón York	ham (cooked)	postre	dessert
judías	beans	primer plato	first course
judías verdes	french beans	pulpo	octopus
jugo	fruit juice	queso	cheese
langosta	lobster	rape	monkfish
leche	milk	relleno	filled/stuffed
lechuga	lettuce	riñones	kidneys
legumbres	pulses	salchicha	sausage
lengua	tongue	salchichón	salami
lenguado	sole	salmón	salmon
limón	lemon	salmonete	red mullet
lomo de cerdo	pork tenderloin	salsa	sauce
mantequilla	butter	seco	dry
manzana	apple	solomillo de	fillet of beef
mariscos	seafood	ternera	
mejillones	mussels	sopa	soup
melocotón	peach	té	tea
melón	melon	tenedor	fork
merluza	hake	ternera	beef
mero	sea bass	tocino	bacon
miel	honey	tortilla española	Spanish omelette
naranja	orange	tortilla francesa	plain omelette
ostra	oyster	trucha	trout
pan	bread	uva	grape
papas arrugadas	Canarian-style	verduras	green vegetables
	boiled potatoes	vino blanco	white wine
patata	potato	vino rosado	rosé wine
patatas fritas fries		vino tinto	red wine
pato	duck	zanahorias	carrots
pepinillo	gherkin	zumo	juice

Road Atlas

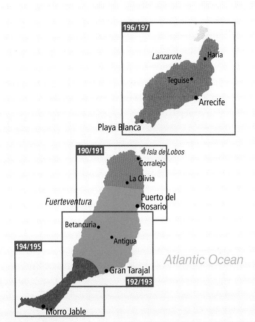

196/197

Lanzarote

Haría

Teguise

Arrecife

Playa Blanca

190/191

Isla de Lobos

Corralejo

La Olivia

Fuerteventura

Puerto del Rosario

Betancuria

Antigua

Atlantic Ocean

194/195

Gran Tarajal

192/193

Morro Jable

Key to Road Atlas

FV-2	Motorway	⚓ ⛵	Harbour; Marina
	Dual carriage way	⛵ ⛵	Windsurfing; Catamaran sailing
FV-10	Thoroughfare	↗	(Swimming) beach
	Main Road	♦ ♦	Monastery; Church, chapel
	Secondary road	♦ ♦	Castle, Fortress; Ruin
	Dirt road	☗ ☗	Radio or TV tower; Lighthouse
	Lane	★ ∴	Point of interest; Archaeological sites
	Path	▲)(∩ ⊓	Peak; Pass; Cave; Lay-by
	Road under construction / development	⛽ ⛳ ✹	Petrol station; Golf course; Windmill
×–×–×–	Road closed to vehicles	⌚ ⚘ ✿	Campground; Lookout point; Oasis
	Tunnel	ℹ ⊕	Information; Hospital
	Ferry	Ⓜ 🎭 ⚑	Museum; Theatre; Monument
	National park; Nature Reserve	✪ ✉	Police station; Post office
	Restricted area	🚃 Ⓑ	Bus station; Bus stop
✈	International airport	Ⓟ Ⓟ	(Multi-storey) Car park; Parking spaces
❷ ★★	TOP 10		
⓫	Don't Miss		
⓬	At Your Leisure		

1 : 600 000

0	10	20 km
0	5	10 mi

5

Punta Blanca
Caleta de Beatriz
Punta Aguda

Punta de la Ballena o de Tostón
Faro de El Tostón [M] **Museo de la**
Pesca Tradicional

Punta de la Enrocadiza

Caletillas

Punta La Barra   Urbanización
Playa de La Concha   Los Lagos
11 El Cotillo   ● **El Roque**   FV-10
Castillo de El Tostón   Mña. La C

4

O c é a n o
A t l á n t i c o

Playa del Castillo

Cerco Prieto

Playa del Aljibe de la Cueva

Playa del Águila
Punta Las Roquecillas

Casas   Blanca
de Taca   308 m

Playa de Esquinzo
Punta de los Caletones

Punta de Paso Chico

Molino   Hoya

Monumento Natural
de la Montaña de Tindaya

Las Gorihuelas   Montaña
Playa de Tebeto   [14] 397
Los Pedregales

Tindaya

3

Playa de la Mujer   M

Playa de Jarugo   Montaña Quemada
294 m
**Monumento de
Unamuno**

Barranco de Jarugo   FV-207   L.

Punta del Salvaje
(El Puerto de) Los Molinos
Playa los Molinos 16   Colonia
García Escámez   Los Mol
Punta de la Vega Vieja   Las Parcelas   **Molino
de Tefía**   Tefía

2

Bahía de las Gaviotas   FV-221   **Ermita
San Ag**
Salinas   Llano de La Laguna
332 m   **7**
C u c h i l l o   d e l   C a b o   Presa de   **Ecomuseo de
La Alcogida**
Puntilla del Agujero   Los Molinos
339 m   Degolla de la
Vista de Casillas   Casillas
355 m   An

Bco. de los Mozos   Tao
Playa de los Mozos   351 m   425 m
Llano   FV-30
Playa de Santa Inés   Aguas   Las Gabias
Verdes   Llanos de la   Los Pasi
Punta de los Caletones   306 m   Concepción   Casas
Morro de Fuente Laja   El Almácigo   San
FV-30   Agustín [M]
Punta del   Valle de   **San Pedro**   Ampuye
Junquillo   Morro Alto   417 m   Santa Inés   Las
190   192   Majadillas
Morro del Junquillo ▲
282 m   Los Cardores   Cruz de las
Ensenada Agua Amarga   Los   Cañadas   FV-20
Punta Gorda   Morro de la Cruz   676 m   Regatones

1

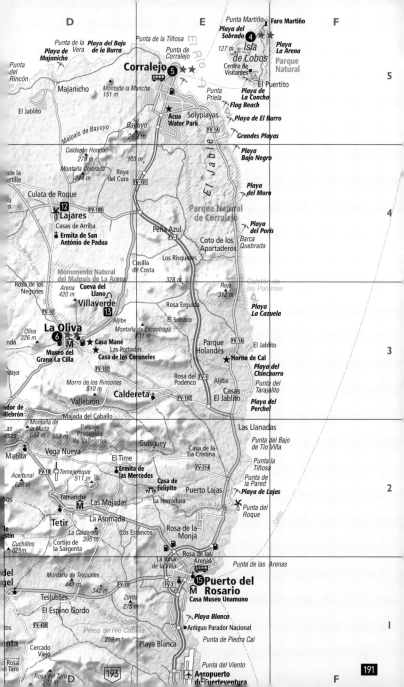

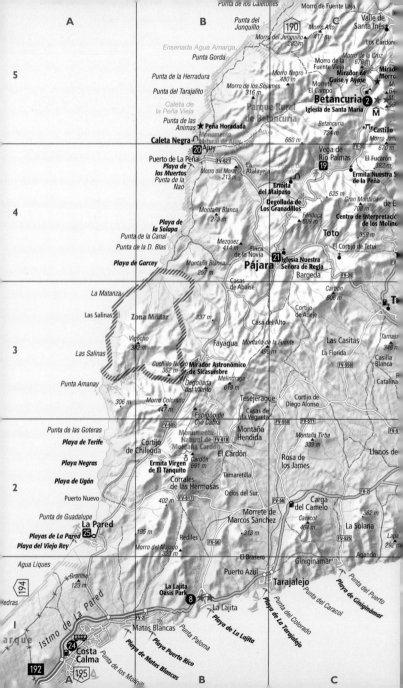

Column A / Top:
Punta de los Caletones · Morro de Fuente Laja · Valle de Santa Inés
Punta del Junquillo · 190 · Morro Alto 417 m · Los Cardon
Ensenada Agua Amarga · Morro del Junquillo 282 m
Punta Gorda · Morro de la Fuente Vieja · Morro de la Cruz 676 m · Mirador Morro
Punta de la Herradura · Morro Negro 480 m · Mirador de Guise y Ayose
Punta del Tarajalito · Morro de los Sojames 316 m · Morrete El Campo · Betancuria
Caleta de la Peña Vieja · Parque Rural de Betancuria · Iglesia de Santa María
Punta de las Ánimas · ★ Peña Horadada · Betancuria 724 m · Castillo · Morro Jan
Caleta Negra · Monumento Natural de Ajuy · 660 m · Morro 670 m

Section 4:
20 Ajuy · FV-621 · Vega de Río Palmas · El Fucarón 392 m
Puerto de La Peña · La Atalayeja · 19 · Ermita Nuestra S. de la Peña
Playa de los Muertos · Morro del Morat 213 m · Ermita del Malpaso · 625 m · Gran Montaña 708 m · de E
Punta de la Nao · Degollada de Los Granadillos · Fenduca 609 m · Centro de Interpretación de los Molino
Montaña Blanca 273 m · Toto 359 m
Playa de la Solapa · Mezquez 414 m · Finca de la Novia · El Cortijo de Tetui
Punta de la Canal · Playa de Garcey · Montaña Blanca 257 m · 21 Pájara · Iglesia Nuestra Señora de Regla · FV-30
Punta de la D. Blas · Bargeda

Section 3:
La Matanza · Casas de Abaise · Carbón 606 m
Las Salinas · Zona Militar · 337 m · Casa del Alto · Cortijo de Adeje
Las Salinas · Vigocho 382 m · Casa del Alto · Las Casitas · Tamasi 346 m
Fayagua · Montaña de la Fuente 496 m · La Florida · Casilla Blanca
Punta Amanay · Cuchillo Negro 362 m · Mirador Astronómico de Sicasumbre · Melindraga 619 m · Cortijo de Diego Alonso · Catalina
306 m · Morro Colorado 447 m · Degollada del Viento · Tesejerague

Section 2:
Punta de las Goteras · Espigón de Ojo Cabra · Casas de la Vegueta
Playa de Terife · Monumento Natural de Montaña Cardón · Montaña Hendida · Montaña Tirba 339 m · Llanos de
Playa Negras · FV-605 · Cortijo de Chilegua · FV-618 · El Cardón · Rosa de los James
Playa de Ugán · Ermita Virgen de El Tanquito · Cardón 691 m · Tamaretilla
Puerto Nuevo · Corrales de las Hermosas · Ocios del Sur · FV-56 · Carga del Camelo · La Solana · Lapa 292 m
Punta de Guadalupe · 402 m · FV-617 · Morrete de Marcos Sánchez · Caracol 464 m · 362 m · FV-525 · Agando
La Pared · 25 · 195 m · 313 m · Rediles · FV-56 · El Brasero · Gingínamar
Playas de La Pared · Morro del Majano 328 m · Puerto Azul · Punta del Puerto
Playa del Viejo Rey

Section 1:
Agua Líques · Granillo 123 m · La Lajita Oasis Park · 8 · Tarajalejo · Playa de Gingínamar
194 · Istmo de La Pared · La Lajita · Playa de La Tarajalejo · Punta del Caracol
edras · FV-2 · Matas Blancas · Punta Paloma · Playa de La Lajita · Punta del Colorado
arque · 192 · 24 · Costa Calma · Playa Puerto Rico · Playa de Matas Blancas · Punta de los Molinu
195

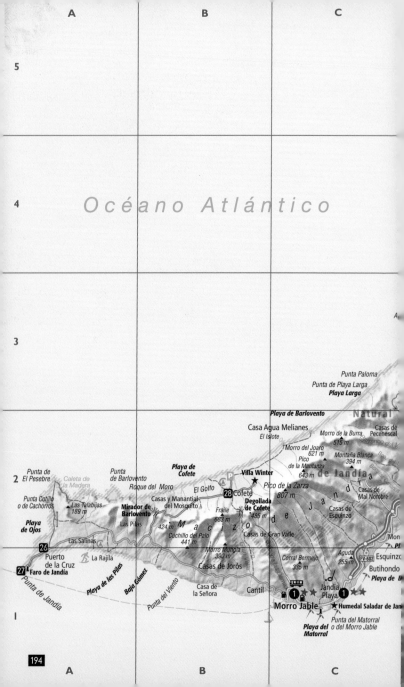

Océano Atlántico

Punta Paloma
Punta de Playa Larga
Playa Larga

Playa de Barlovento

Natural

Casa Agua Melianes
El Islote

Morro de la Burra
515 m

Casas de
Pecenescal

**Playa de
Cofete**

Morro del Joaro
621 m

Montaña Blanca
394 m

Punta de
El Pesebre

Caleta de
la Madera

Punta
de Barlovento

Roque del Moro

Villa Winter

Pico
de la Mantanza
643 m

de Jandía

28 Cofete

Punta Cotillo
o de Cachorros

El Golfo

Pico de la Zarza
807 m

Casas de
Mal Nombre

Casas y Manantial
del Mosquito

**Degollada
de Cofete**
485 m

Las Talabijas
189 m

**Mirador de
Barlovento**

Casas de
Esquinzo

**Playa
de Ojos**

Fraile
683 m

d e   J a n d í

Las Pilas

424 m

Cuchillo del Palo
441 m

Casas de Gran Valle

M a c i z o

Las Salinas

Mon

26

La Rajila

Morro Mungla
390 m

Corral Bermejo
335 m

Aguda
255 m

FV-602

Esquinzo

27 Faro de Jandía

Puerto
de la Cruz

Playa de las Pilas

Bajo Gómez

Casas de Jorós

Butihondo

Playa de B

Punta de Jandía

Punta del Viento

Casa de
la Señora

Cantil

Jandía
Playa **1**

1

Morro Jable

Humedal Saladar de Jan

Punta del Matorral
o del Morro Jable

**Playa del
Matorral**

194

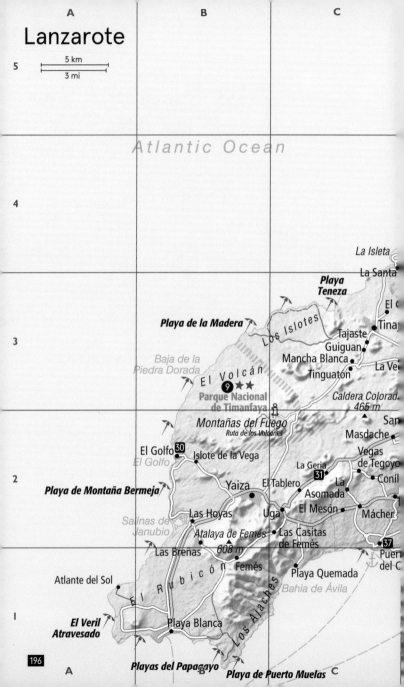

Lanzarote

5 km
3 mi

Atlantic Ocean

La Isleta
La Santa
Playa Teneza
El c
Tina
Playa de la Madera
Los Islotes
Tajaste
Guiguan
Baja de la Piedra Dorada
Mancha Blanca
La Ve
El Volcán
Tinguatón
Caldera Colorad.
465 m
Parque Nacional de Timanfaya
San
Montañas del Fuego
Ruta de los Volcanes
Masdache
El Golfo
Islote de la Vega
Vegas de Tegoyo
El Golfo
La Geria
Conil
Yaiza
El Tablero
La
Playa de Montaña Bermeja
Asomada
El Mesón
Mácher
Salinas de Janubio
Las Hoyas
Uga
Atalaya de Femés
608 m
Las Casitas de Femés
Las Brenas
Femés
Puer del C
Atlante del Sol
Playa Quemada
Bahía de Ávila
El Rubicón
Los Ajaches
El Veril Atravesado
Playa Blanca
196

Playas del Papagayo
Playa de Puerto Muelas

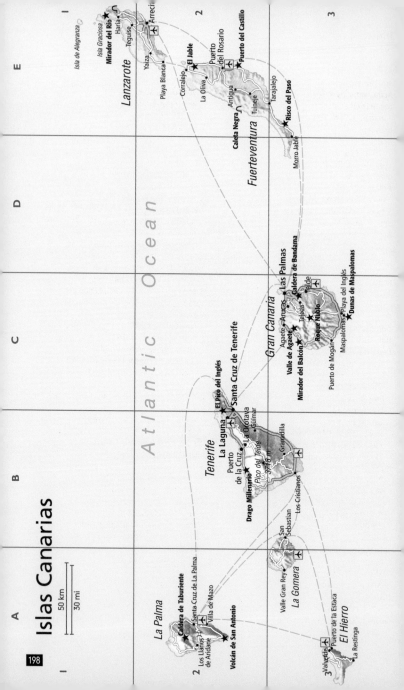

198

Islas Canarias

50 km
30 mi

Atlantic Ocean

La Palma
Caldera de Taburiente
Los Llanos de Aridane
Santa Cruz de La Palma
Villa de Mazo
Volcán de San Antonio

La Gomera
Valle Gran Rey
San Sebastián

El Hierro
Valverde
Puerto de la Estaca
La Restinga

Tenerife
Puerto de la Cruz
La Laguna
La Orotava
Güímar
Drago Milenario
Pico del Teide 3718 m
Granadilla
Los Cristianos
El Pico del Inglés
Santa Cruz de Tenerife

Gran Canaria
Agaete
Arucas
Las Palmas
Telde
Valle de Agaete
Mirador del Balcón
Roque Nublo
Caldera de Bandama
Puerto de Mogán
Maspalomas
Playa del Inglés
Dunas de Maspalomas

Lanzarote
Isla de Alegranza
Isla Graciosa
Mirador del Río
Haría
Teguise
Arrecife
Yaiza
Playa Blanca
Corralejo
La Oliva
Puerto del Rosario
El Jable
Puerto del Castillo

Fuerteventura
Antigua
Tuineje
Tarajalejo
Caleta Negra
Risco del Paso
Morro Jable

I
E   D   C   B   A

1   2   3

Index

Picture Credits

AA: Steve Day 172; Clive Sawyer 30, 125; James A. Tims 50, 52, 57, 59, 84, 108, 162, 164; Steve Watkins 37

akg: Album/Oronoz 18

DuMont Bildarchiv: 20; Gerald Hänel 5 (bottom), 9 (top), 19, 21, 22 (top), 24 (bottom), 29 (top right), 31, 74–75, 75 (right), 82 and 6 (3), 87, 104 (left), 105 (right), 106 (top right), 106 (bottom right), 114, 120, 134, 135 (right), 136, 142–143, 155, 156, 185; Sabine Lubenow 5 (top), 14–15, 16, 29 (top left), 29 (bottom), 36, 45, 49 and 6 (4), 51 and 6 (5), 53, 54, 55 and 6 (6), 68–69, 73 (top right), 74 (top left), 77 (right), 78 (top) and 6 (2), 81, 89, 90, 91, 92–93, 96, 98–99, 103 (top right), 109, 110 and 6 (1), 112, 113 and 6 (8), 117, 123, 127 (top), 127 (bottom), 128–129, 133 (top right), 134–135 (top), 138, 139 and 6 (10), 140, 144, 146, 149, 150, 151, 152, 154, 160, 167, 168, 171; Olaf Lumma 19 (top), 43 (top left), 43 (bottom), 44 (bottom left), 104–105, 116, 145, 148; Hans Zaglitsch 26, 76–77 (top)

laif: 141; Aurora/D. Santiago Garcia 44 (top left); Hedda Eid 73 (top left), 94; Gerald Hänel 56; hemis/Pierre Jacques 166; Naftali Hilger 24 (bottom), 76 (bottom left); Julia Knop 44 (centre right), 44 (top left), 66, 67; Robertharding/Markus Lange 83; Tophoven 121

Look: age fotostock 9 (bottom); Aurora Photos 22–23 (centre top), 23 (bottom); Alex Tino Friedel 22–23 (centre bottom), 111; Bernhard Limberger 118, 158–159; Sabine Lubenow 12–13, 38–39, 137; Brigitte Merz 46–47, 76–77 (bottom), 119 (bottom); Jürgen Richter 32; Thomas Stankiewicz 176–177; travelstock 44 58

mauritius images: age fotostock/Juan Carlos Munoz 43 (top right), 76 (top left); age fotostock/Martin Siepmann 10 (top); Alamy 35 (bottom); Alamy/AA World Travel Library 25; Alamy/CW Images 46 (left); Alamy/geogphoto 27, 44 (bottom right); Alamy/mastix 133 (bottom); Alamy/philipus 103 (top left); Alamy/Lynne Sutherland 10 (bottom); Alamy/travelstock 44 106–107; Reinhard Eisele 174; Manfred Habel 62; Rainer Hackenberg 60; imageBroker/Siepmann 65, 88; imageBroker/Michael Weber 61; P. Kaczynski 134–135 (bottom); united Archives/Werner Otto 133 (top left); united artists 175

© VG Bild-Kunst, Bonn (César Manrique) 2018: 5 (bottom), 142–143, 151, 154, 156

On the cover: Sabine Lubenow/Lookphotos (top); Stephen Dorey/Getty Images (bottom)
On the back cover: Marco Simoni/Getty Images

Credits

2nd Edition 2020
Fully revised and redesigned

Worldwide Distribution: Marco Polo Travel Publishing Ltd
Pinewood, Chineham Business Park
Crockford Lane, Chineham
Basingstoke, Hampshire RG24 8AL, United Kingdom
© MAIRDUMONT GmbH & Co. KG, Ostfildern

Authors: Rolf Goetz, Paul Murphy
Editor: CLP · Carlo Lauer & Partner, Valley
Revised editing and translation: Christopher Wynne, Bad Tölz
Design: CYCLUS · Visuelle Kommunikation, Stuttgart
Project manager: Dieter Luippold
Programme supervisor: Birgit Borowski
Chief editor: Rainer Eisenschmid

Cartography: © MAIRDUMONT GmbH & Co. KG, Ostfildern
3D illustrations: jangled nerves, Stuttgart

Printed in Poland

Despite all of our authors' thorough research, errors can creep in.
The publishers do not accept any liability for this. Whether you
want to praise us, alert us to errors or give us a personal tip –
please don't hesitate to email or post:

MARCO POLO Travel Publishing Ltd
Pinewood, Chineham Business Park
Crockford Lane, Chineham
Basingstoke, Hampshire RG24 8AL
United Kingdom
Email: sales@marcopolouk.com

FSC
www.fsc.org
MIX
Paper from
responsible sources
FSC® C018236